ANONYMOUSLY FAMOUS ™

Mira Tzur

"I can't even count the times I talked about the business with a thirsty girl, guy, or kid eager to know more about the industry and their chance to be part of it; wishing I could just hand them this book. Anonymously Famous™ is finally here for all of you.

A great pleasure in life is doing what people say you can't."

~Mira Tzur

Enigami & Rednow Publishers, New York
© 2020 Mira Tzur
All rights reserved.
ISBN-13 978-1945674518

This is an interactive book. Please download the **Quick Scan** QR Code scanning application or use your smart phone camera to get the full experience.

Mira Tzur

Dedication

I would like to dedicate this book to all the souls that influenced my life choices and stood by my side at every intersection to guide me or distract me—consequently, to point me in the right direction at any given moment.

And as I once told Harvey Weinstein, who admonished me for sitting in front of him at the Tony awards, "It's not who you are, Mr. W, it's who you know"

Mira Tzur

Model: a person or thing regarded as an excellent example of a specified quality.

"as she grew older, she became a model of self-control"

a person, employed to display clothes by wearing them.
"a fashion model"
synonyms:
fashion model, supermodel, mannequin
"a runway model"

a person employed to pose for an artist, photographer, or sculptor.
- synonyms:
- subject, poser, sitter "an artist's model"

Something that a copy can be based on because it is an extremely good example of its type:

TABLE OF CONTENTS

Mira Tzur

PREFACE

Anonymously Famous™ is a master-guide to the world of commercial print lifestyle modeling as an everlasting odyssey rather than a short-lived career.

In this informative A to Z guide, I illustrate my own—often humorous—25-year experiences and journey through the industry and demonstrate that modeling is a lifestyle that evolves with you not away from you as time goes by.

While most fashion modeling books speak to the 1% population dreaming of pursuing the unattained dream of becoming a supermodel, this book speaks to the other 99% that, at one point in their life, had a desire to brush with the modeling world but didn't think they could. The target audience is anyone who still dreams of working in this business decade after decade.

The idea or I should say, the misconception that a model's career comes with an expiration date is one of the reasons I have decided to write this book. No one should determine when you should end your career but you. That is true for any career you happen to have, including modeling.

I have also written this book as a guide to help individuals interested in the print and commercial modeling business to understand better what they need to do to achieve success. Most importantly, it is a way of demonstrating that a model's age can be an advantage, not a disadvantage. I have devoted considerable space and provided my own experiences and expertise as someone who had used each milestone in my life to increase the longevity of this beautiful ongoing career.

In writing this book, I have sought out individuals who, like myself, have overcome the stereotype and the fallacies about who should and can be a part of our industry. They share their tips, advice, and stories within the pages of this book.

I believe "Anonymously Famous™" is a germane reflection of where our society is headed by its current social media movement, where our culture doesn't value anonymity for too long. If you aren't showing on a google search, you either don't exist or you're not relevant.

I have also incorporated a token of my extensive background in health, fitness, and nutrition, sharing the evolving needs for the different activities based on your dynamic age ranges or state of mind.

Furthermore, this ultimate guide will demystify this industry; for that reason, I shied away from focusing on the fashion arena as it is often short-lived and long talked about. I'd rather focus on encouraging youngsters and mature individuals to taste this American dream and the lucrative world of advertising.

The world of commercial lifestyle demonstrates a strong message that, at every age, we should be a model of example (examples shouldn't be taken only at a younger age). I believe that 20 years of experience is a far higher value than 20 years of age, even in a business that is driven by external beauty. That aside, elaborating over the differences between; print, commercial, voice-over, hosting, animation, unions, agents, managers, casting directors, makeup artists, models; fit, foot, fitness, part, petite, plus, mature, etc., can make the difference in pursuing one.

PROLOGUE

"Why don't you stick to dancing, Mira? You're very talented, but photogenic you're not."

Those words broke the heart of my then 15-year-old self, a wannabe model coming off her first disastrous photo shoot. That negative sentiment carried with me throughout my adolescence, and I focused on dance, as suggested, and shelved my dreams of becoming a model.

In the mid-1980s, my father had a prominent graphic design business in Israel, where top consumer magazines would hire him for their design needs. His line of work for these publications might have been partially responsible for triggering my desire to grace those glossy pages. But when my father finally set-up my first photoshoot, I was sorry to hear their input and suggestion that I stick to dancing. Please don't get the wrong impression; my father was very supportive and cared for my dreams but didn't want to see me struggle to achieve this farfetched profession. Here I was, with an open-door to the industry, but unable to walk through it.

You see, it was way before iPhone Mania, so taking selfies and submitting them for castings was not even in the conceptual womb. It was a different time when young girls did have to rely on so-called professionals to dictate their career choice, approve their desire, and match their talent. It's mind-blowing to think how much authority we gave others to shape our careers and hold us back from our dreams. This is especially true in comparison to today's world, where anyone can pursue their dream to become something, with no approval needed, promoting their assets, and building followers and popularity.

I never asked for another test-shoot, nor did I mention my hidden desire to model. But, as fate stepped in years later, I was approached by a prominent active apparel group-Everlast worldwide to be their spokesmodel & presenter, based on my dance background and athletic assets. When the student is ready, the teacher appears.

So, as I incorporated modeling into my life for more than two and a half decades, I realized that as much as I enjoy this full-time/part-time career, when asked about what I do, the answer is never straightforward. "I do commercial print lifestyle-modeling, consumer ads, and lifestyle-advertising." This statement is usually met by a puzzled look followed by, "What is that? Are you a photographer? Do you have an advertising agency? You mean you're a model?"

Such moments do need a thorough explanation when you're over forty. I try to explain that modeling isn't just for young girls but is an actual profession that grows with you over time. No matter what age I hit, I try to be the perfect "model"/example for that decade. Being in this space makes me strive for my "perfect me" at any age. I see modeling as timeless, limitless, and everlasting as long as one can lead-by-example. I certainly try to be my best, daily.

I decided to write this behind-the-scenes book after helping hundreds of people navigate this business and launch their careers. It's something that comes organically to me as I love this industry and want others to share its rewards. Even though this business requires a more in-depth inner look for increased self-awareness and growth, I often marvel at watching how many people find their identity and self-love as a result of their modeling pursuits. I hope this book is an extension of that. I seek to share my broad experience and expertise, incorporating insights from colleagues and industry professionals, creating a comprehensive guidebook to commercial print lifestyle modeling. Hopefully, Anonymously Famous™ will serve as a launchpad into this magical industry.

INTRODUCTION

Most people's vision of a model is a sixteen-year-old genetic wonder of nature with legs to the sky. They strut runways and stare at you from the pages of glossy magazines. By 25, their careers are over as the next round of underage beauties takes their place. I'm here to tell you there's a whole other side to the modeling world, one that lasts a lifetime and develops with you over the decades. Let me introduce you to the world of Commercial Print Lifestyle Modeling.

I look forward to breaking down the many branches of this business and explaining how to successfully approach each category so you can maximize your talent, profit, and time. In this profession, you are your business. The better you understand your type, your market, and how to present yourself, the more likely this will become a viable career for you.

Even though I'm in my forties, I'm consistently working as a model, now more than ever. I began realizing that at each stage of my life, there are demands for my evolving look. Few careers are so adaptable. I felt that by sharing my experiences and exposing the secrets of this fascinating industry, I could help others pursue their dreams—rather than them giving up or finding excuses why they don't fit the widespread misperceptions of the modeling world.

My first brush with modeling came during my childhood in Israel; It was a disaster. As an accomplished ballet dancer, I knew how to move on stage, take direction, and use the space, but in front of a camera, it was a different story. As I mentioned, my father worked in advertising, and after relentlessly begging him, he connected me with a prominent photographer to do my first test shoot. The pictures were horrible, and it registered deeply in my mind as a failure. What I didn't realize was that one shoot did not determine my career nor my future. No matter how attractive you are or aren't, being photographed is like working your muscles. It takes practice to get the photos you need. After all, practice does make perfect—as does a photographer that knows how to capture your best angles on camera.

It didn't help my ego that by the time she was three years old, my blonde hair, blue-eyed sister had already been the face on a baby-doll package and was considered "the pretty one" during our youth. Scan the QR and see my point.

That experience stuck with me throughout the years and served as a driving force to better myself and accelerate my talents.

Graduating from *Thelma Yellin Performing Arts School* with a scholarship from the *America-Israel Cultural Foundation*, my career as a dancer flourished, forcing my pursuit of modeling onto the back burner. But the desire always

lingered; I knew that chapter wasn't closed. I joined the *Batsheva Dance Ensemble*, and during those years, I served the Israeli military as a counterintelligence officer before moving to New York at the age of 20.

Living in New York, the Mecca of theater, Broadway beckoned. I began pursuing work in musical theater. I danced both on and off-Broadway and traveled with various productions across Europe. From the royal stage of Monte Carlo to the Antwerp Belgium opera house, to King Hassan, the second royal palace in Marrakech. My dancing career and associations attracted the attention of numerous fitness apparel companies. Before I knew it, I was offered a contract as a spokesmodel/presenter with Everlast; a relationship that lasted more than seven years. All of a sudden, I was a model!

I still felt awkward calling myself a model and always made sure to emphasize I was a "fitness" model as if that wasn't real modeling. The Everlast contract inspired me to become a certified fitness trainer and nutritionist, which opened other doors to health & wellness. Such collaboration was one of many others that came over the years, including; *Nike, Capezio, Jacques Moret, Reebok, Head, Converse, Vitamin Shoppe, NY Sports Club, Equinox, Weight Watchers, Zone, SlimFast,* and many more.

When I became pregnant, like most women in my profession, I worried that my career would falter with the arrival of my son. It turns out that "Mommy & Me" was the next phase in my modeling career. *Toys R'Us, Safety First, Huggies, Disney, and Buy Buy Baby* were just a few. I quickly added to my portfolio as a new parent. Unfortunately, my son never developed the same passion for modeling and instead focused on athletics; so, I continued shoots with different children of varying age groups. Of course, I am happy for him as he stayed determined and achieved the highest level of sports playing lacrosse and football in college.

I was now approaching thirty and began to see my job offers shift. My looks matured, and I was well-suited for more corporate campaigns for the likes of *IBM, Canon, Sony, Dropbox, Citibank, Bank of America, US Bank,* and other luxury hotel brands as *Renaissance, Four Seasons, Trump Marina, and Hilton.* Even now, in my mid-forties, I continue to work consistently.

By now, it should be evident that this industry offers endless opportunities over a lifetime. Suffice it to say; I am looking forward to becoming the new face of *Depends* and representing the latest arthritis medications, *Viagra, AARP,* and many more in my later years.

I hope to inspire you to jump-start your career; if this is a life that you find exciting, you will learn that this industry can offer endless possibilities for your unique journey.

Commercial portfolio

Fitness portfolio

CHAPTER ONE

—FASHION AND COMMERCIAL MODELING—
The key differences

A re you interested in getting into the modeling world? Do you know what category into which you fit? This chapter will provide you with information about the main differences between fashion and commercial modeling.

—FASHION MODELS—

Fashion models are hired to display designers' fashions to entice consumers and buyers to purchase their goods. They showcase the designers' collections on the runway, in showrooms, and fashion magazines.

These models must be tall and slender (5'9 to 6'1) often young, and with unique looks. While there are some shorter, very successful fashion models— Twiggy, the first short supermodel from the '60s and Kate Moss being the most famous at under 5'7—the industry tends to lean more towards taller statures. High fashion models must be a sample size, which means that you must meet height and measurement requirements to work in the major markets. These girls usually weigh-in between 90 and 120 pounds, depending on height.

High fashion models must also be young. The industry standard age range for fashion models is usually between 13 and 25 years old. Agents prefer that models launch their careers in early teen years to compete with the high fashion international marketplace. This requires the minor's parents to chaperone while traveling abroad. Europe's main high-fashion capitals are Milan, Paris, and London, and all offer significant opportunities in editorial and runway work. Of course, Brazil, Tokyo, Canada, and Spain are great work locations, but the rules change from country to country or state to state. These markets offer more opportunities for catalog and commercial advertising work.

—COMMERCIAL PRINT MODEL—

The people you see in catalogs, advertisements, billboards, and packaging, fall into the category of commercial print models. While high fashion comes with many limitations ranging from age and height to weight and bone structure, commercial print is a little more forgiving and often highly lucrative. Models can be shorter, average weight, and either 'real' looking, or 'great beauties'. Age restrictions don't exist in commercial print; there are work opportunities for people ages 1 to 99.

Personality and the ability to believably portray a role is essential in commercial modeling as you will often be acting real-life situations. Unique traits and improvisational skills are a significant asset. Quite possibly, you will find yourself shooting an everyday scenario, like eating at Olive Garden with a good-looking matched family or newlyweds frolicking on the beach at the latest couples resort, miming a presentation speech in a well-designed boardroom, or playing a doctor writing a patient's prescription. There are many types of creative activities this job can require.

I look forward to sharing the many aspects of this ever-growing industry.

—TIPS AND CONSIDERATIONS—

Most modeling agencies have different major divisions, created for both fashion models and commercial print models. If your agency represents both segments, you will likely be represented in one category but not the other. For instance, you may be signed to the fashion division, commercial print division, or "across the board'. At larger agencies, different agents for the individual divisions may represent you. With the rapid growth of reality TV, lifestyle personalities, and celebrity endorsements, agencies have developed additional categories ranging from mature, celebrity, 'real people', international, influencers, lifestyle-parts, athletes, and competitive fitness. By finding your niche, you can aim for the proper representation in all the markets in which you may work.

Keep in mind; modeling agencies are extremely selective with the models they represent as they must meet the needs of their clients and follow market trends. To do this, modeling agencies must represent models that fit the client's demographic. With that in mind, if an agency does not sign you, it may not mean that you cannot model. It simply means that you are not a good fit for their specific market, or that your portfolio is not strong enough at that particular time. Don't be discouraged; revisit, update, and upgrade your brand and images.

—ANDY PEEKE—

"All-American" Male Model Interview

"One of my favorite things to happen on set is when I'm just hanging out with the other talent, and the photographer starts shooting us because our interactions are happening so naturally. Then the photographer says, 'Thanks, we are all done,' and I'm thinking, 'when did we even get started?' "Those shoots are great because of the chemistry."
~Andy Peeke.

Q: When did you start modeling? What inspired you to start?

A: I started just after college. I contacted a talent agency in Denver, and I was doing my first shoot with Sports Authority a week later. I always knew I wanted to model. I used to wash my parent's cars with my shirt off while growing up in Los Angeles and thinking, "maybe a model scout/agent will come by and see me, and I'll be discovered." My dad had some moderate success as a model and a commercial actor in the 1970's.

Q: What did your first portfolio contain, and how many test shoots versus editorial and ad campaigns were included?

A: My first book consisted of one test shoot.

Q: What advice do you have for aspiring models?

A: Do what you love. If what you love changes over time, that's fine, but don't keep doing this if you're not enjoying it.

Q: How often do you do test shoots to provide current images, and how many agencies are you with?

A: Oy Vey, I'm not going to answer that because you might call me a whore. I test a few times a year, and I try to always communicate with the photographer about the kind of images I'm looking to get from that test.

Q: You are considered the "All-American" classical type. How has your look/background helped you conquer the market, and what age range do you target?

A: Sometimes, being "All-American" is a blessing and sometimes a curse. It's all about what a client is looking for. I find it important to show up and be myself. Hopefully, the client will like me and book me. It sucks to work in an industry where you have to rely on hope so much. Often, I'll go on a casting, and a client will say, "We love your look, and you would be great for us." A few times, I've responded with, "Great, then how about you end the casting and book me for this job." It worked once.

Q: Name three of your most exciting jobs, and what sets them apart?

A: They were so exciting that I've probably forgotten. Shooting an episode of "Million Dollar Listing" was a lot of fun. I sat in a hot tub with three other models and sipped champagne for three hours. I was the last person to leave set because I was having so much fun. Shooting with Bruce Weber is always entertaining, we've done campaigns for Polo and A&F together.

Q: You've had a successful career that's spanned decades. Describe how this profession has influenced your lifestyle over the years?

A: I focus on eating right and staying in shape. I try to keep up with fashion trends, so I don't look like a dork, but it still happens.

Q: What role does fitness and diet play in your life?

A: Diet is huge for me. But I prefer the phrase "food intake." I've had strong opinions about eating healthy since I was a child. I have an obese mother, and I've always been at odds with her regarding health and nutrition.

Q: Is it fair to say that you are in charge of your career, regardless of how many agents or managers you have? Specifically, when it comes to bookkeeping, submissions, and material updates, is it your constant job to provide?

A: Yes. I'm mostly in charge of my career. I can accept or pass on jobs as I please. A couple of years ago, I finally informed my agents that I'm no longer willing to do tobacco ads. Also, I don't model real fur because of animal cruelty. I strive to have synergy with my agents so we can optimize our efforts.

—HEIDI LINDGREN—

"All American" Fashion Model Interview

"You need to learn very early how not to take anything personally."
~Heidi Lindgren

Q: When did you start modeling? What inspired you to get started?

A: I started modeling at the age of 13 when I got chased down at a Britney Spears concert by my soon-to-be agent from Irene Marie Model Management. My mother was not a fan of the idea. Still, after speaking to Irene (a mother herself) who had been a staple in the industry for years, we decided to give it a try.

Q: What did your first portfolio contain, and how many test shoots versus editorial or ad campaigns were included?

A: The contract that I signed with Irene Marie dictated that no costs were to be incurred on my part. The agency would put up the money for me to start testing and filling out my portfolio. That way, I could work with quality photographers, stylists, hair, and makeup artists who would increase my likelihood of acquiring work. As I worked, the money advanced to me would be deducted from my check, interest-free, until I paid back the agency. I genuinely believe this is the only way to operate. I always tell people to never, ever pay for anything upfront. If a legitimate agency wants to sign you and believes that you will work, they will front the costs to get you started.

Q: *How many agencies are you currently with, and how often do you test shoot to provide current images?*

A: I'm currently placed with eight agencies across the world (with only one in the United States). I now have reached a point where I rely on recent editorials and ads for my portfolio and generally no longer test. If I do free shoots with photographer friends, it is for ourselves and not for my book.

Q: *What advice do you have for aspiring models entering the fashion world at a younger age?*

A: You need to learn very early on not to take anything personally. Modeling is one of the only industries in which you are hired based on something you can do very little about; your genetics. If you take it personally when someone does not book you—or even if they make comments about your looks to your face, which does happen since you can sometimes be treated as more of an object than a human—you will go crazy. It's a bit like dating— you have to realize that just because you aren't right for one client doesn't mean there isn't a surplus of other clients out there who would love you.

Q: *You are considered the "All-American" classical type. How has your look/background helped you conquer the market you are in, and what age range do you target?*

A: Age range has never been something I've considered. It varies a lot depending on the client, and my agents are the ones that decide whether I should go out for specific jobs if I would fit the part. My "look" has always been an interesting point for clients because the vast majority of them assume that I am Nordic. It's always a surprise when I show up with my very American accent and personality.

Q: *Name three of your most exciting jobs/accounts, and what sets them apart?*

A: Shooting the Guess by Marciano campaigns was by far the most exciting point of my career. Guess is just such an iconic brand, and they always work

with the best of the best. They produce the most beautiful images, and the productions are always so incredible and over the top. It makes you feel like you are on top of the world. The same goes for shooting the cover of GQ in South Africa. We shot the editorial inside but had no way of knowing what the cover would be until they released the magazine. The day I found out that we got the cover will always be one of my favorite memories! I have to say that earning Talbots as a client has also been one of my favorite things.

They really have become a family and shoot such fun, beautiful, lighthearted images – I always look forward to a day on set with them!

Q: You've had a successful career that allowed you excessive traveling. Describe how this profession has influenced your lifestyle and choices over the years?

A: While it's amazing to be able to travel to so many places, it can take its toll on you. One of the hardest parts for me was adjusting to an utterly inconsistent life. It's very difficult to make plans for yourself or with others when you never know if you will have to jump on a plane and leave the country. I have learned to surround myself with people that are understanding of this aspect of my life and supportive of me. Additionally, trying to keep as much consistency as possible—such as reading my devotional and meditating every morning when I wake up, no matter where I am—has helped me maintain a sense of balance in an industry that can often leave you feeling off-kilter and exhausted.

Q: What role does fitness and diet play in your life, any secrets to share?

A: As I always say, the secret to fitness is that there is no secret. Hard work is the only answer, and your work will reflect your level of dedication. I have my ups and downs, but having someone you are close with that will check in with you and be honest helps a lot.

Q: As a fashion model with several agencies all over the world, you are sure in charge of managing your career and schedule. How important is it to keep track of all your bookkeeping, submissions, and material updates; is it fair to say that it's your constant job to provide?

A: I leave all of this up to my mother and agency, Muse Models. They do an amazing job of communicating with all of my other agencies, coordinating jobs and trips, collecting images, being respectful of my personal life, and scheduling things that are important to me. I feel communication is key here. It is important to have a mother agent that you trust, and that will give you honest feedback and listen to your concerns.

CHAPTER TWO

—TYPES OF COMMERCIAL PRINT LIFESTYLE MODELING—

—PRINT/STILL PHOTOGRAPHY—

P rint images are still photos used to represent an item, company, or brand, ranging from fashion to pharmaceutical, and fitness to finance. Your photo could be used on anything; brochures, tags, packaging, billboards, internet ads, consumer magazines, and whatever other media the tech geeks invent over the coming years. For print bookings you'll agree to an hourly or day rate plus a usage fee for the images (we'll go into more detail on this later).

—STOCK PHOTOGRAPHY—

An additional form of print modeling, stock photography, is an option for those just getting their feet wet in the industry. Stock photography, in most cases, means you are signing away your rights to the photos. This allows the photographer to sell your images to any outlet in the years to come. Typically, you get paid a day or hourly rate, but should your photos be used in any media, you're not entitled to additional compensation.

There are two main categories for stock photography image use: royalty-free and rights-managed. Royalty-free means that anybody can buy the image at the same time, so there is no brand conflict or exclusivity. Royalty-free images are less costly. Rights-managed means the image is bought outright, which is far more expensive but valuable to the company.

Early in my career, I wanted to update the photos in my book and decided to do a stock session. Years later, I received an excited call from my son's nanny, who was traveling in Romania at the time. She'd seen a picture of my toddler son and me on an *Orangina–Cappy* vending machine, an image taken years before. Of course, I'd signed away my rights to the image, and I didn't see another dime—but my exposure in Romania was spectacular.

Another time I was in the Metro train station and saw an enormous poster of myself in an *Atkin's* ad. Flattering? Yes, profitable? No!

Recently, my now teenaged son sent me a nice text message, "Thanks for embarrassing me again, mom." He added a link to the daily newspaper with an article titled, *Lead by Example*, that showed a picture of a well-dressed soccer mom next to a mom who wore her

pajamas on the morning school run. That same image was also used on a highway billboard years earlier in an ad saying, "Buckle up, it's the law," and for packaging of a Bluetooth device. See these examples by scanning the code. Notice the different colors of our shirts, and where did my turtleneck go?

The list of these instances is endless for many models that do stock photography – be prepared to see these images in random places for years to come!

—ANTOINE VERGLAS—

International fashion photographer interview

Q: What was your career turning point or the moment you realized you could make a living as a fashion photographer?

A: Having, in my humble opinion, a pretty good photography story idea and managing to meet a key person who believed in me and what I was trying to achieve

Q: It is fair to say that you contributed to some of the most notable names becoming famous, shooting lots of magazines covers with them all over the world. What would you say is different now than in the supermodel era?

A: I am not sure who helped who at what time, but I was helped at my early stage. Today the world is different in fashion photography. It came in three different steps ;

A. The internationalization of magazines with multiple international editions for every publication bringing to the forefront new talented international photographers and the need of celebrities on covers or models turned supermodel celebs

B. The digitalization of the photographic world, the speed, the computers, the cost—everything became different during a shoot, and you can see results immediately. Everybody can look at it.

C. Smartphones and social media, instant viewing of shoots behind the scenes, basically nothing can be kept secret any longer. The developing time of Polaroids and films being the next day or so. No more surprises, no more mystery. I think the legacy of fashion photographers such as David Bailey, Terry O'Neill, Guy Bourdin, Richard Avedon, Helmut Newton, Irving Penn, to name a few, no longer exist in the same way as they did.

Q: Who are your favorite models of all time to work with, and what makes them special?

A: There are many. I was a big fan of Stephanie Seymour, Heidi Klum, Claudia Schiffer, Adriana Lima, Linda Evangelista, and Alessandra Ambrosio for different reasons and depending on what I was asked to work on.

Q: You are known to capture candid, natural, sexy shots. Does being French in the American market, play a role in your creative decision making?

A: I think it's always an asset at the beginning to be a foreigner in a market you want to infiltrate. You bring your unique cultural background, vision, and expertise in a certain way, creating freshness, comparing to what the mainstream is doing. Even today, as the world is changing so much and people travel a lot more in the early stages.

Q: Can you name two or three projects that were forever memorable or stood out during the process?

A: A French Elle, documentary-style cover project, Sports Illustrated swimsuit cover story, calendars with Claudia S. Heidi K. and elite models. GQ covers in the USA and international editions, as well as later Maxim US and all over the world. And, of course, Victoria's Secret, being my client for roughly 20 years

Q: If you had to give one piece of advice to an aspiring model, younger, older, taller, or shorter, what would it be moving forward on her passion?

A: Nowadays, becoming a successful model is a harder task than 30 years ago. It requires multiple skills in front of a camera, starting with attitude and an exuberant personality. Elocution, presence, look, and allure are much more crucial when using a video camera. These days, they are the way we go as they have become more relevant than still photography.

—THE LATE DAVID GARVEY—

Photographer Interview

"Retouching is more prevalent in the industry than ever before because with the availability of photoshop, software and filters, just about anyone can do it. It has become a business of illusion more so than ever before"
~David Garvey

Q. What are the ten most important images for a model to have in a commercial portfolio vs. fashion portfolio?

A. The basic image package for a commercial portfolio should contain various looks. For example, the headshots should be a variety of expressive emotions from smiling, to sadness, to worrisome, to relaxed. These can be mixed with lifestyle scenarios such as interaction with street vendors, talking on a cell phone, or simply hailing a cab. They should include business, upscale, and casual attire in their photos. It's about coming across as believable as can be in any given scenario. When it comes to Intimate apparel and lingerie, it should be shot with a demure, soft attitude rather than sexual. The difference would be in expression, pose, and choice of lighting. For fashion models, though, it's a lot about how you wear the clothes, especially for catalogs, unique lighting, and more aloof expression is useful.

Q. What should a model expect at the test shoot?

A. Test shoots are an integral part of the modeling industry, whether they are new to the business or experienced veterans looking to update their look. The most important thing about a test shoot is having a predetermined plan as to what you want to achieve. This is established between photographer and model before the actual shoot. The model should expect to visually convey the ideas previously agreed on. The photographer is expected to capture the moment, so the session is beneficial; in most cases showing up with no game plan can be a waste of time.

Q. How much input do models have in choosing their looks?

A. The amount of input a model has in determining his/her look would depend largely on the degree of experience she/he has. A new model would, most likely, receive guidance from people in her agency. The bookers know what clients are looking for and will let the new people know what kind of images they need to effectively market them. A more experienced person acquires a feeling of what works for him/her and will usually collaborate with the photographer to get the idea right.

Q. How much do you rely on retouching and photo enhancement in postproduction?

A. Retouching is more prevalent in the industry than ever before because with the availability of photoshop, software, and filters, just about anyone can do it. It has become a business of illusion more so than ever before. Under-eye-line, facial blemishes, and pores have virtually disappeared. While we all use it to different extents, it's extremely important not to overdo it to where the subject becomes unbelievable. Excesses in retouching have prompted casting directors to do "Polaroids and digitals" of people at the casting to get an accurate idea of what they look like pre-booking.

Q. What's your personal preference, shooting indoor or outdoor? Please explain the pros and cons of both.

A. I enjoy shooting both indoors and outdoors for different reasons. Indoors, whether it be the studio or location, I control the environment, the lights, the props, etc. Outside, however, you have to be a better photographer because you have to deal with variables like the weather and circumstances around the shoot. Shooting on the streets of New York, for example, can be an adventure depending on when and where. On shoots in places like the Virgin Islands, we usually had to deal with unpredictable weather conditions, and because of cost factors finding a way to get the shoot done meant rethinking background and light options. In other words, when on location, having a "plan B" is a must.

Q. How much influence do you have on the art director and client? Do they utilize your expertise and value your input?

A. I always listen to what the art director and client have to say. The client knows how he wants his brand represented. The art director has taken the client's input and has developed a plan to convey that message. I'm expected to create the visualization through lighting and direction. If they have a comment during this process, I respectfully listen. If I didn't think it will work, I'd tell them why; it's a synergistic relationship.

Q. Name three of your best jobs, and what sets them apart?

A. I've had many jobs I've enjoyed over my thirty-plus years.

These are three that come to mind; A Ray-Ban campaign we shot together, the cast and team were fun to work with, and we all got to keep all the eyewear we used. Feeling Great magazine was another, it only lasted about five years, but we did a lot of international location shoots. I was also allowed to do Pope John Paul's portrait during his US visit in 1995. It was truly a spiritual experience I'll never forget.

—FITNESS MODELS—

At 26, I signed my first contract with Everlast Apparel Group and got my feet wet in the modeling industry. Becoming a fitness and nutrition spokesmodel was an organic extension of my professional dance career. I represented Converse, The Jacques Moret Group, and was the Everlast Woman presenter.

A fitness model is not necessarily a professional athlete; being in top shape is a prerequisite – a workout routine, good night's sleep, and a healthy diet are vital for this very competitive segment of the industry. You're never fit enough to rest on your laurels. Many fitness models also take part in body figure competitions and parts modeling, which we'll discuss later.

If you happen to be a professional athlete who becomes known, that's great, since you may find yourself inking major endorsement deals. Think Linsey Vonn, Tiger Woods, Tom Brady, LeBron James, Roger Federer, and countless others whose athletic success has become synonymous with a certain brand. LeBron James' lifetime deal with Nike and Air Jordan. Maria Sharapova with Tag Heuer watches, and Canon-Power-Shot. Odell Beckham for Nike, Pedialyte, and Dunkin'

Donuts; to name a few.

However, even if you're not a professional, having the basic skills in a variety of sports can come super handy at the fitness castings. You may be put on the spot to do a yoga pose, handstand, jump rope, or any other type of sports action that a job you audition for may require. The other must-do is knowing how to pose – it should be your top priority to show off your physique at its best since the casting sessions are usually very short. You might only get one or two shots to leave behind for the client to review, so practice in the mirror. I remember struggling to find my best angles, but once I did, it made a world of difference. *See shape images in the QR at the beginning of the chapter.

My time spent in the studio as a ballet dancer was certainly helpful. Like an actor memorizing their lines, I had to learn my most photogenic angles. Of course, having a spray tan before a body-conscious shoot never hurts when scantily clad—it helps to highlight muscle definition, evens skin tone, and gives a nice healthy glow. It's like Airbrush Makeup for your body.

Sometimes you get lucky with a great makeup artist and a younger Adonis posing next to you, like in the story of the ad for Slendertone. Those rock-hard abs were a combination of fitness and great makeup artistry—we looked like we lived at the gym. The point here is that makeup, and a tan can enhance your assets, but it's your responsibility to keep yourself camera ready and in workable condition.

There are lots of notable Anonymously Famous™ fitness models, especially now, saturating the social media platforms, but a few years back when I worked with fitness model Jelena Abbou, on some Gym equipment and running machines, I remember her chiseled body gracing the cover of Oxygen, Self, and Fitness magazine. We talked about her vigorous diet and training for her next bodybuilding competition and the three different divisions one can actually compete: Figure, Physique, and Bikini, which requires each, a different training, definition, body type, and overall shape. In all cases, hardcore training and discipline is a must.

Men also thrive in fitness modeling, cultivating lucrative careers flaunting their chiseled abs and muscular glutes on the covers of magazines, supplement companies, and fitness equipment—often inspiring real bodybuilders to steal their choice of angles and image compositions. Many of them carry out their online training routine and courses specifically to get into the perfect shape and secure followers. From Lazar Angelov the bodybuilder known for his best abs, to Mike O'Hearn, TV model and fitness star who launched quite early his fit plan app for training and nutrition to Brett Azar who happened to play Arnold Schwarzenegger's body double in the Terminator installment, Terminator Genisys, and was then promoted to play the role of young Arnold.

—ANDREW FOORD—

Commercial Photographer Interview

"When making a presentation, remember that you are a storyteller. First and foremost, you need an engaging narrative. Secondly, keep it light and fun"
~Andrew Foord

Q: You've always been a generous photographer with your time and knowledge. Your latest efforts include showing your behind the scenes and how you light on your Instagram feed. How has this notion of pay it forward helped your career?

A: That's an interesting question because, on the surface, it seems a bit backward. How has helping others advanced my career? One example of my paying it forward is my recommendation of creatives and brands that I work with— whether it be photo-assistants, models, makeup artists, hairstylists, fashion-designers, set-designers, lighting equipment, camera equipment, etc. Instagram, for example, is a massive player in the world today. Simply tagging someone can open doors that otherwise might have remained closed.

Q: Has it ever hindered you in any way?

A: To be honest, I'm not sure if I've ever lost a job because of tagging an assistant. If I had, it was because they were the better choice, for whatever reasons, for that particular job.

Q: Where does your desire to pay it forward stem from?

A: I'm compelled to mentor and advise other photographers and assistants because I wasn't traditionally mentored. I had significant figures advise me against pursuing photography for a living. If I can give any insights or help any light bulbs go off, I'm happy to do it.

Q: Do you feel having a family-culture in the industry benefits you, if so, how?

A: Creating a supportive community of producers, assistants, and crew is essential. We have a lot of fun on set, even though we are working hard and putting in long hours. My crew isn't afraid to point me in a different direction or make recommendations that will improve my images. I know how talented my crew is and do whatever I can to be equally supportive of them. On my set, everyone has a voice.

Q: You've always been successful, lately, even more so. What do you attribute this new level of success to?

A: I honestly don't see myself as "more" successful than I have been in the past. If anything, I feel like I am still on the hunt to be successful. My measure of success is on a per-shoot basis.

There are still clients for whom I haven't worked and subjects that I haven't photographed. I am very fortunate to work for a number of clients, which gives the impression that I'm everywhere, but I have dry spells and setbacks just like everyone else. Even at my level, there is still more to accomplish.

Q: Tell us three key things you keep in mind for client presentations, creative meetings, and keeping people engaged.

A: The best thing to do when you're making a presentation is to remember that you are a storyteller. First and foremost, you need an engaging narrative. Secondly, keep it light and fun. Make 'em laugh. Finally, do your homework—know what you're talking about. Otherwise, why should anyone listen?

Q: What are five key things for any young photographer getting into the business to keep in mind?

A: 1: Stay focused. Yes, it's hard, but anything worth doing is worth doing right. 2: Stay organized. Run a tight ship. Stay balanced. 3: Work hard and play hard. 4: Make it easy for your clients. They are more stressed then you are. Anything you can do to simplify the process will ultimately help you. 5: Act like a professional and bring old-school graciousness to our profession.

Q: How often do you promote yourself?

A: I share photos on Instagram daily. Word of mouth, mailers, and emails are all excellent tools for promotion, but being able to post an image in 30 seconds, which will direct a potential client to my online portfolio and booking page is amazing.

Q: Do you view photography as a technical vehicle to practice your craft or a creative vehicle to express it?

A: That's a good question. For me, creativity always comes first, but you need to have the technical knowledge to pull off the ideas. It's a lot more involved than simply pressing the shutter button, same goes to the model, it is so important to be confident in front of the lens. You could be the most beautiful/handsome model, but if you lack confidence with yourself or the photographer, it will show. Chemistry and the joy to make every shoot a creative process is key to any successful shoot.

—MATT KARAS—

Photographer for Dancers / Athletes Interview

Q: You are known to be one of the top photographers specializing in capturing movement and motion. How is working with dancers and athletes different from shooting models, and what kind of equipment and techniques are needed to create such shots?

A: In my experience, working with dancers, and athletes provide different opportunities, compared to working with models. When I work with both groups, 'story' is always important to allow the subject to be present and convey a story or narrative. It can be a relationship between two dancers or two models in love and happy. There's a large number of relationship possibilities, but the most important thing is that they are connected. Dancers and athletes have their physical disciplines that allow them to control their bodies in either a lyrical movement or an explosive, energetic motion.

Both dancers and athletes train their bodies using repetitive exercises—getting stronger and trying to obtain a certain type of perfection in their bodies and their movement. Dancers are trying to get their bodies into an exact shape to achieve a classical pose in ballet, for example, or repeating a pose from a particular choreographer. The athlete manipulates their body in whatever way necessary to complete the play. On the other hand, models have learned to use their bodies to express the emotion of a situation, sometimes using stillness, just with the way they carry their head, balance their weight, manipulate their arms, and hands or use their eyes to help tell the story. There is a nuance in how they use all the muscles in their faces to bring a spark of life, a searing look that cuts through, up close the camera can catch and portray. Where dancers use their bodies to tell a story in motion, it is the model's job to use the positioning of their body itself as the narrative.

I am freezing people in motion for some of my work, both commercial and fine art photography. To capture this extraordinary motion, keeping it crystal clear without blur is a challenge to overcome. When I first began creating, I used light to stop the action rather than the camera—usually 1/2000th of a second. Imagine if you take one second and split it into 2000 pieces and take just one sliver of time. Over the last four years, technology has caught up. You can now use the camera's shutter to stop the movement. I shoot with Hasselblad, Canon, and Fuji cameras utilizing Broncolor lighting equipment and Profoto too. Regarding shooting models, I use the same equipment, but the timing of the camera and lights may change to create many different effects or moods.

Q: What are some of your pet peeves working with models /dancers, and what preparations do they need to take before shooting with you?

A: I consider myself blessed to have had so many wonderful experiences with dancers, athletes, and models. I always try and connect with my subjects before they step in front of my camera. When the models are having makeup and hair done, or the time it takes dancers to stretch to warm up, I ask many questions and get to know as much as I can from them directly. In every shoot I am involved with, I also research each subject I will be shooting. Lastly, laughing is the most important part of the day—joking around is essential; I like to keep my sets upbeat and lively. One thing to note, even though I enjoy being humorous with people, I am always taking the job seriously and am dedicated to making the end product exceed the client's expectations.

Q: Tell me a bit about your background and how you paved the way to the specialty work you do?

A: As a hobby, my father's passion for photography got me going. I started taking pictures at 15-years-old. In the first seventeen years of my career, I spent as an actor and director. I was working in regional theaters and off-Broadway. A health challenge changed my course, and I transitioned to international sales of translations for websites and software. Throughout these years, I always enjoyed taking photos and using a camera. Then I pivoted to medicine, working at Mount Sinai Hospital as a cardiovascular ultrasound tech; after three years in medicine, my desire to be creative needed an outlet. I changed careers for the last time and decided to do photography full time. I started working for different photographers and then two years later began sharing a studio with another photographer. What I found was that my experience as a director and actor would be a vital tool allowing me to work with both professionals and people with no experience in front of the camera. I was shooting dancers while freezing them in motion and started to get my work in front of different art buyers and editors. I was disciplined in approaching companies and individuals to follow up and gain exposure. Shooting outside and freezing subjects was not easy when I began. This was one of the factors that put me above the rest.

Q: Please share with us the type of clients and assignments you get to work on and how much creative freedom you have vs. the talent?

A: The Kennedy Center in Washington, DC, is one of my favorite clients. I have been privileged to provide advertising photography, a number of their season brochures & marketing campaigns for productions, including billboards, buses, print magazines, newspapers, and theater programs. We have shot together for The Kennedy Center Dance Season and The Washington National Opera's 60th Anniversary season. In these shoots, I worked closely with the Creative Director of the Kennedy Center, and we plan months in advance because the talent we need to photograph may only be available one or two days during the year due to their schedules.

Working with Dance Magazine, I had the opportunity to photograph over 50 covers. They used both established stars and up & coming performers who have gone on to stardom, for example, Misty Copland from American Ballet Theater and Tiler Peck from New York City Ballet.

With the magazine covers, we had to provide at least four cover images and at least 7-10 images for the inside of the magazine or online.

For five years, I photographed the CEO of iHeart Radio, Bob Pittman. This job allowed me all-access to the incredible two-day super shows in Las Vegas, running around backstage with musical legends like Prince, Paul McCartney, Usher, Jennifer Lopez, Justin Timberlake, Lady Gaga, Arianna Grande, Green Day, and many others. This type of client is a run and gun—you are constantly moving and have to create moments directing the musicians while hustling to capture candid moments.

Q: What percentage do you emphasize on getting the exact shot you want vs. fixing it in post-production?

A: Much of my work is about precision and capturing the peak moment when everything is together and tells the story. I strive to capture the images in-camera, so there is little retouching to be done later. I think it is lazy when photographers or ad clients say, "we will just fix it in Photoshop." If you choose that path, you will spend more money on post-production. I love the challenge of inspiring the talent to achieve our initial goals.

Q: Having a studio in the center of town in NYC, the mecca of all performing arts and Broadway stars—who are some of the great names and companies you have worked with, and how is their professionalism made a difference in the outcome?

A: I have had the pleasure of working with many terrific individuals who were total professionals and made our shoots a tremendous experience. Getting to work with Emily Blunt, who was very funny and kind. Liev Schreiber, Adrien Brody, and Michael Strahan were all very entertaining but focused. Andy Blankenbuehler, who choreographed Hamilton and many others on Broadway, was the most prepared subject I have ever shot. He worked for days on his own before we worked together to have endless moves for a magazine story. There were 15 images published in the magazine story. That was far more than they expected to run. Julianne Moore was the most gracious to me, my entire crew, and everyone on set that day. I must admit, you, (referring to the author, Mira Tzur), are a professional through and through who is dedicated to the work both in front of the camera and behind the scenes. You're always prepared and ready to work to get the shot, whatever it takes. You work tirelessly to help connect people you know and people you meet to help make work happen. As a producer, you pull people from your network and team them up to make projects happen. I am honored you asked me to contribute to this book.

—ALEXANDRA APJAROVA—

Aerial Artist, Model, Choreographer Interview

"Because my main focus was on dance and aerial arts, my print career was more of a dance modeling with a commercial twist."
~Alexandra Apjarova

Q: Tell us about your professional background?

A: I started as a rhythmic gymnast and became the National Champion of my native Slovakia right after I transferred to dance and choreography. Since I am a dreamer, I wanted to challenge myself in the big city. I arrived in NYC in the summer of 1994. My first dance gig was in the Russian style cabaret I was making $50 per night in Brighton Beach. But my first aerial work appeared when I joined Anti-Gravity in "Barnum Musical."

Luckily, I continued to work with them as a rhythmic dancer, actor, and model. This led me to my contracts with Cirque du Soleil's Delirium, Michael Jackson's, This is It, Leona Lewis's Labyrinth Tour, award-winning Off-Broadway show, La Soiree, and other high-end productions. With such in place, the modeling job opportunities came towards me.

Q: Have you seen modeling and dance coincide in your professional experience?

A: Yes, definitely, I had a few agents. One focused mostly on my dance bookings and some print castings. The others had more on-camera commercial castings, which was always a bit harder to book. However, because my main focus was always on dance and aerial arts, I was able to stand out and book lots of print campaigns and on-camera dance commercials.

Q: What are your dietary habits, and how does nutrition impact your performance?

A: I eat everything but try to keep my carb intake low and focus more on protein and vegetables. I make sure to have a good breakfast and lunch and moderate my portion for dinner. Water and sleep are very important, and I love to sleep. The more I'm dancing, the better shape I'm in and burn so many calories that diet hasn't been a big problem.

Q: What's your fitness routine?

A: Practicing Aerial work forces me to use my body weight, which is a vigorous and challenging form of exercise, also cardio is very important. I dance combinations over and over until I'm sweaty and tired. I also teach in NYC!

Q: How does being a mother impact your work? Any mommy and me jobs?

A: Of course, being a mom makes it harder balancing childcare, but I'm able to juggle it pretty well. I'm a little more limited, but it's still possible to work and continue my career. My son just turned 6-years-old, so now I can bring him along, depending on the job.

Q: Name 3 of your most exciting jobs besides Cirque du Soleil, Michael Jackson, or La Soiree?

A: Well, all of the above were iconic production experiences for me and really exciting, because I love what I do. But there are a few one-time event highlights that I performed with Anti-Gravity such as the Obama Inauguration Ball, Grammy Awards, Victoria's Secret Fashion Show, Smash, Winter Olympic Games, cover of "Dance Spirit," spread in "Shape" magazines and much more.

Q: What advice do you have for aspiring performers?

A: I am a perfect example of coming from a foreign country to the US to follow my dreams. Take a chance, work hard, spread your wings, and don't give up!

Q: Are you in any unions, and how do they impact your career?

A: I got into SAG-AFTRA when I booked "Just My Luck," the movie director Donald Petrie gave me a role called "sky dancer," and I was able to join right away. Previously before that, I did some events for Good Morning America and others that gave me waivers. I've had credits for stunt work on TV shows like Smash, Victoria Secret Fashion Show. I was featured in Say Yes to the Dress on TLC.

—FIT MODELS—

Here's a category that many people have never heard of but can be extremely lucrative and fill the days when print jobs are slow. For this category, it's your measurements that matter. Whether you're a size 2 or size 14, it's all about your proportions being true to that size, so designers can accurately make a fit sample consistent with the industry standard. Unlike on-camera work, in fit, the bigger your size, the more work is available. This is also a fantastic option for plus-sized women. You'll try on the full collection in front of the designer tech team, and they'll analyze the fit when the garment is on-body, making notes. I know this sounds easy, but you're on your feet all day with very little downtime.

This is a great category for more mature models since the designers want your feedback on the garment's feel and cut. Once you've done it long enough, the terminology becomes second nature. This makes you a real asset to the company and can result in the coveted long-term contract. If you do sign a contract take this seriously, it's a bond between you and the company, and they expect your sizes to remain the same for the line to be sized consistently. Though this may not sound as appealing as modeling swimwear in Fiji, I call it the "Golden Hanger" for a reason. You're essentially a hanger making up to $250 an hour, sometimes for as long as 10-12 hours a day regularly.

It's always good to know whether the brand you're casting for uses American or European sizes. Americans generally run a little larger, in which case it's okay not to hold your stomach in when they measure the waist. It sounds crazy, but that inch can determine whether or not you get the account.

—THE ART OF THE MANNEQUIN—

Fit Fat Foot Fetish & Creation of the body double

To discuss Fit Modeling, it is important to explore the history, which began with the use of mannequins—also known as "lay figures" or "body doubles."

Mannequins date back as early as ancient Egypt, where King Tut used them to hang, fit, and display garments. Later the French and Dutch term figurine was adopted and still used today as stand-ins for live models

One of the pioneers in this field of figurines is Ralph Pucci, who evolved the look and image to what we know as the modern mannequin. Pucci was able to breathe life into those mannequins and depicted their shapes and forms year after year to fit societal changes, preferences, and ideals of beauty, depicting the latest fashion trends.

Pucci's mannequins are not mere clothes hangers; they are true works of art reflecting society trends, curated for exhibits in the Tiffany & Co Foundation Jewelry Gallery, the lobby of MAD magazine headquarters and even a collaboration with fashion icons like Diane Von Furstenberg and Christy Turlington. According to Ralph Pucci, "over the years, my role is to create exciting mannequins that are reflective of the time we live in."

During the 20th and 21st centuries, the use of live models became the standard. However, with the escalating costs and the growth of technology in computer-generated body imaging, we are beginning to see the use of mannequins again. Natural-looking mannequins can be easily imaged from real people resulting in the loss of work for live models.

I experienced this change. I signed a lucrative fit modeling contract with a major maternity-wear company in Philadelphia. I wore a prosthetic belly to simulate the first trimester of pregnancy. For several months I traveled back and forth from NYC to Philadelphia for long day fit-sessions. However, for the second season, my contract was bought outright. My measurements were taken to create a mannequin of me ending my contract. The mannequin stole my job!

—SHOWROOM MODELS—

As a showroom model, your job is to present the collection in the best possible way so the buyers will be tempted to place large orders to sell in their department stores or on their websites. Sometimes, you'll be frantically changing clothes; other times, you'll be bored out of your mind, sitting in the model's closet waiting for the next buyer to arrive. So, take a book, or if you're an aspiring actor, this a great place to go over your lines.

The busiest time for a showroom model is during market week, when buyers come to town from all over the country, and sometimes the world, to view next season's collections. There are typically four major market weeks per year for various segments of the industry, including bridal, couture, swim, lingerie, eyewear, and others.

Always be presentable and friendly at showroom jobs. Your presence and positive attitude will be a major factor in selling the product. Occasionally buyers will ask your opinion about a garment; make sure that feedback going to the designer is measured and constructive. As for the buyer, always find something positive that encourages them to place an order and make your design tech team look great.

—PLUS-SIZE MODELS—

This category has become increasingly popular as American retailers are realizing that their customer base is, on average, a size 14, according to recent research. A size 12 consumer will not identify with a size 2 model, "she" wants to see the garment she's interested in purchasing on someone that represents her size and shape. Whether you're a size 10 or 18, you can find work in this category, but you must be well proportioned. As a general rule, when measuring, there should be about a three-inch difference from your bust to your hips, no matter what size you are. You can see the size chart below for reference.

Women's Size Chart (American Sizes)

	XS	S	M	L	XL	1X	2X
Dress Size	0	2-4	6-8	10-12	14-16	18-20	22-24
Bust	32-33	33.5-35.5	36-38	38.5-40.5	41-43	44-47.5	48-51.5
Waist	25.5-26.5	27-30.5	31-33	33.5-35.5	36-39	39.5-42	42.5-45
Hips	33.5-34.5	35-37.5	38-40.5	41-43	43.5-45.5	46-49.5	50-53.5

Men's Size Chart (American Sizes)

	XS	S	M	L	XL	XXL	XXXL
Neck	13-13.5	14-14.5	15-15.5	16-16.5	17-17.5	18-18.5	19-19.5
Chest	33-34	35-37	38-40	42-44	46-48	50-52	54-56
Sleeve	31.5-32	32.5-33	33.5-34	34.5-35	35.5-36	36-36.5	36.5-37
Waist	27-28	29-31	32-34	36-38	40-42	44-46	50-52

*All measurements in inches

—BICOASTAL MANAGEMENT, FIT AGENCY—

Founder, Malissa Young Interview

While Bicoastal Management was founded as a Fit Model agency by a former pro fit model, it has grown into a full service agency with headquarters in both NYC and LA: Fit is still a massive portion of the business and a source of pride for owner and founder, Malissa Young.

Q: Can you share the work you do as a Fit agency with your models vs. as a commercial print agency?

A: As a fit agency, we are more likely to see our models sporadically throughout the year as they update photos and measurements since the fit business is so measurement specific. For example, if a size 4 gains 1 inch in circumference on her chest/waist/hip, half an inch on thigh and bicep, she is now categorized as a size 6; as the grade between sizes 2, 4, 6, 8 is only 1 inch. Sometimes a model takes up a new fitness routine that changes her shape. Spin classes, for instance, seem to shrink waists while increasing hip and thigh. We also have fit models or budding fit models in for model training. Pro fit models are like an additional tech designer who gives comments very specifically, so we need to provide a basic foundation for newer models to have a chance to build a career. Once a model is working steadily, we know their measurements are maintaining, so we may not see them for over a year as we handle the schedule and invoicing via email and phone/text.

Q: How can one get started, knowing if she/he has the right fit size to pursue such a career, and does age and looks matter, or only the dress size and true measurements?

A: It has a bit of a complicated answer in some areas. One can get started by finding a fit representative or looking at online ads for in-house fit model jobs. Some fit models have taken pattern making classes to get a better understanding of garment structure. Some also work as personal trainers while they are getting established, or print/commercial models. If clothes tend to fit you perfectly, you are the right size. If you have noticed shoulders on jackets are always tight, but bust and waist are perfect, you are probably too broad in the shoulder. Or if you are noticing your back rise often dips, your bootie is probably too full; unless we find you a smaller niche curvy fit account. While there are general standards, there are always brands doing exception fits like curvy, muscular, tall, or petite. Regarding age, there is not really an age limit, but it is easier to break into the industry before reaching the mature stage because if a client has an older customer and indeed wants a fit model whose over 45 to be their model, they will be casting many models who have ten or twenty years' experience. If you are new, even with the perfect specs, one of these other seasoned fit models will probably also have the perfect specs, but they will have a resume and knowledge base that helps them get the job. Also, if a model is in the more mature market/brands targeting women 40-70, the designer often has a say in who is picked, and being a designer, often with a more visual mind, they will often say they want someone aspirational and inspirational to them in the fitting. While it may not be specifically stated, we often see that means someone gets the account a bit on the younger end of the age range. Exceptions are 1. Established relationships with designers. Some consider models friends and muses and will keep them working well into the older years for modeling. 2. Experience and knowledge. Some companies will want that model's 30 years of experience speaking up and guiding in their fittings. So while I don't mean to sound against at all, I hope to give an honest review based on my experience. Fit models can work into their 60s very successfully. I have seen this on a few occasions, but they didn't start at 50; more likely, they started in their 30s or younger.

Q: What are the set proportional measurements for each typical working size? How did they change through the years and which are the most desirable among your clients nowadays? Please elaborate on the trends and designers using certain sizes & body types.

A: To give a few target measurements, we see often:

Women M-height 5'7-5'8
Size 4: 34.5-27-37.5,
Size 6: 35.5-28-38.5

Men M-height: 5'11"- 6.' 40 chest, 32 waist, 18" down from the high point of shoulder, seat 40, inseam 32.

In all cases, there is wiggle room usually up or down ½".

Some clients will have a straighter body shape in mind, some more muscular, curvier, thinner, or fuller, and tend to vary. Some trends I have seen since I started fit modeling in the late 90s are the targeted height has gone down for women. We see some clients asking for 5'6'-5'7" and fewer clients opting for a 5'9" model. Sizes have become more generous. Today's 6 was a size 8 twenty years ago. For men's fit, some brands don't stick to the above target specs but also look for wider midsections, and conversely, some who look for more muscular fits as well.

Q: What should one expect when going on a fit-go-see or a showroom go-see and how important is it to know the lingo and add your comments to the design team session vs. keeping it to yourself?

A: For a go-see, you want to be diplomatic, so offer comments when asked, and make them related to fit, not the design. If you want to compliment the design, by all means, do. But don't say you wish it were shorter, longer, different neckline, etc. You can say, it feels balanced or fits very evenly, or if it is a little tight or loose, point that out diplomatically. For instance, "This dress fits me perfectly through the shoulder, chest, waist, sweep, but I do feel the low hip could increase just half an inch more to make it more comfortable for walking and sitting." They want to see you will contribute to their having a great fitting garment. For the showroom, the feedback is less important. You are there to help them sell the garment and make it look good. Focus on positives and have a bag of tricks, perhaps to make it fit as good as can be—padded bra, minimizer, waist shaper, etc. They will worry about the fit later after getting the sales.

Q: How important is it for a model to stay consistent with her/his measurements, and how often do you need to remeasure and update the profile for accuracy with your ongoing client requests?

A: Once you have an account, they expect you to stay the same size. ¼" up or down is a half-inch range and considered normal; what the industry calls tolerance. One inch is often a whole size grade. I prefer a scale every morning, and giving a 3-pound range to know specs are staying steady. Some models prefer a tape measure check, but tapes can stretch; as can the measurer —sometimes we want to convince ourselves nothing changed so you pull tighter or hold looser allowing more margin of error.

Q: How important is it for talent to be exclusive to your agency vs. freelance working with multiple agencies in your field, and how often can they be booked on fit hours a week?

A: There is too much competition in too small a niche for most agencies to consider signing a model freelance. The ones who do are usually starting out, don't have as many accounts to offer access to yet, and just need to build a board to build their business. We have all been there. I have been exclusive for 95% of our fit model signs for the last several years—meaning after year 3 in business. By having one agency, you are, as a model, maintaining that you are submitted consistently as one set of measurements. I had a model for years that had two other agencies. We have had some success together, but when she came back from maternity, and we were all trying to rebuild her book, I had one client say, "I don't want to see her again; everyone is submitting her." So my advice is to have one good agency; one you can communicate with who you can ask, "Where have I been submitted?" Or, "How about these brands I wear; do you work with them?" Also, perhaps a two-year contract rather than 3. Trust your gut and trust reviews.

Q: Please share a few of your favorite bookings or stories that managed to set them apart and keep them forever memorable.

A: Oh my goodness, personally as a fit model, some of my favorites stories are getting to travel with the Marc Jacobs fit team to India, Poland, and Sri Lanka to work with factories. I worked with lovely ladies who were a pleasure to travel with and saw parts of the world I probably would not have. I also worked for some designers that kept things dramatic and everyone on their toes. My worst, but also a most memorable story, is coming off of stomach flu and shifting a fitting to afternoon to be sure I was well. There is always a sense of urgency and deadline, and a desire to keep clients happy, so you keep them. I was fitting for Vera Wang bridal at the time; the most gorgeous elaborate gowns, and I thought I was well. I sipped a peppermint tea on my way there for a little energy, but halfway through the fitting, I knew it would not stay down. I let my team know, and someone started shouting, "The dress, the dress," and I was quickly unzipped to hop across the giant skirt in my underwear and throw up in a basket in a corner. They sent me home promptly.

Being a fit model is a wonderful career. You can make a great living, working consistently for decades, getting paid to travel while, to some extent, setting your own hours as well. We have models who work 10-6 on average, with slow weeks here and there, or some who work 6-8 hours but make enough to have that as their main source of income and free time to pursue other passions.

—NICOLE LEBRIS—

Plus Size Model Interview

Q: What inspired you to pursue modeling?

A: I'm not sure. I was kind of obsessed with the 90's supermodels when I was in high school. I subscribed to Top Model. Does it even exist anymore? There were also many magazines that had all the latest shots of the hottest models such as Nikki Taylor, Cindy Crawford, Naomi Campbell, and Kate Moss, and the list went on.

I personally never thought I could model. I was never the skinny type, ever! I also didn't consider myself attractive. But I knew deep down that I was interesting looking because people would make comments to my parents when I was younger. It was hard to look at myself objectively, so I didn't know what to think of myself, and it was kind of up and down for me for a long time. But my weight and size was definitely something that occupied lots of my mind – I never felt confident. With time, as I got into doing hair/makeup work in the industry, I fell in love with the aesthetics aspect of the fashion industry. I'd be working with photographers that said, "Hey, you could be doing some plus-size modeling." So the seed was planted early in my hair/makeup career. I was pretty shy and reserved, so I didn't think I was made to be in the spotlight; it freezes me up. Having said that, I decided to send in my pictures to a few agencies I found online that had a plus-size model division, and the first one took me in. I did a photoshoot and started to work with them immediately.

Q: How does plus-size modeling compare to straight-size modeling?

A: We get to eat and indulge a bit more without the constant pressure to stay thin! I've been around enough straight-size models to see most of them don't get to eat much and walk hungry all day, especially the younger girls. I guess the older models are more into commercial print and acting, so it's different. But the younger girls are constantly being told to trim down or lose weight. I kept thinking to myself, "I don't see any fat on their body. Where will it come off from if they do?" It's always been a bit absurd to me. When I find myself at a casting that is mixed type, the plus-sized girls are always the loudest, vivacious, and most comfortable. I guess leaning towards the straight-size girls, they all seem to be moodier and aloof. We always joke that it's because they haven't eaten in days; maybe it is, maybe it isn't, but I know the pressure they have to stay thin can make some of them very miserable inside. I also believe that it's a lot more competitive and cutthroat due to the numbers. For us plus-size models, we aren't as many, and we all tend to know each other.

Q: How many agencies do you work with, and was it difficult to find representation?

A: I've worked with a few over the years, some for a shorter time than others. I've been with Dorothy Combs Models now for about ten years. Before her, I was with Model Service. I've also been with Images and Muse in NYC.

Q: How often do you test shoot?

A: I test a few times a year as my agent constantly says, 'you get back what you put in.' If I want her to market me to a new client that does classy, sexy lingerie, I better go out and do a test shoot in classy, sexy lingerie so I can show them how I would fit their brand. This is also another way that the straight-size modeling world is different from plus-size modeling. Lots of new photographers use straight-size models as their muse to present their work, so these are free tests for the models. Normally there are not as many photographers that would use a plus model for their portfolios. But this is definately shifting these days with few known names that dropped major awareness and acceptance to the average size, between the Kardashian phenomena to Ashley Graham. However, we are still the minority in the fashion industry, which is absurd since it's a 21 billion dollar industry, and as of 2016, Plus size American women are 67% of the population. The category is growing significantly faster than the overall apparel market

Q: What type of jobs do you usually book?

A: I do mostly E-commerce and Catalogues. My clients are Lane Bryant, Macy's, Shopko, Belk, Kohl's, Fruit of the Loom. I've also shot a few on-camera commercials for them.

Q: What have been your three most favorite bookings?

A: One of my favorite memories was at my earlier stages when I shot a *Fruit of the Loom* campaign. Not only did that job get me out of debt, but it also kick-started my career. Of course, that boosted my confidence immensely. There were lots of people on set and other top models; I remember thinking, "This is what this business is all about." Everyone was so nice. Styling, hair & makeup, catering, a dozen people from the advertising agency, and the clients. It was one of the biggest shoots I've done in NYC. It was giving me the legitimacy I needed then, that indeed, I'm a model. Another fun one was for *Lane Bryant*. I went on a casting for the campaign, and all the top working models were there. I felt like I had no shot of booking it, but on my way home, my agent called me to say I was booked. I was thrilled as I beat up the competition. I was one of the few they chose. That gave me the extra validation I needed. I have what it takes to continue.

Q: What is your fitness and nutrition regime?

A: I don't have a fitness routine I can say I'm committed to, but I always try to make healthier choices with the little things such as choosing stairs over elevators and walking over driving. Sometimes I take a class with friends at the gym or head up to my mom's and go for a hike with our dogs. I try to incorporate being active into my everyday life. No one can call me lazy; that's for sure! About two years ago, I even ran a half marathon. A friend mentioned it, and I thought, why not. She ended up not running due to an injury, but I continued with my plan, which was hard for me. I've never considered myself a runner, perhaps a light jogger. So that commitment was big, and of course, when I finished, I felt such a sense of accomplishment.

Q: Sports Illustrated used plus-sized models in their most recent swimsuit edition, do you think that exposure has helped shed a positive light on your industry segment?

A: I think every exposure in the matter helps, although the model used was quite slim and for most readers would not be recognized as a plus-size model. It's still a step in the right direction, though. They also used a larger model who's a true size 14, but unfortunately, that was still a paid advertisement, not their choice. However, it's great to see plus-size models on any magazine that sets the tone in the industry. I hope it'll keep coming as I wished I had more examples to identify with growing up. I probably wouldn't have struggled with my confidence as much had I known it was ok to be a plus.

Q: Do you feel campaigns like Dove and the book Curves have helped accept women of all sizes, or do you think there's still judgment out there?

A: I think there's always going to be some judgment, but thankfully because of these campaigns, it's a lot more acceptable nowadays. It sure helps that fashion icons like the Kardashians, J.Lo and Beyoncé are shifting from the straight size towards plus size—it's very important for the younger generation to grow up comfortably in their skin whatever size that might be.

—PETITE MODELS—

Don't be discouraged if you are not measuring in at 5'10. There is a market for 'petite' or 'small' models – though you'll never hear an agent use the word short – whose heights range from 5'3-5'7. Models in this category get a lot of lingerie and swimwear work. Parts modeling and shoe modeling (where sample sizes are 6.5-7) as well as beauty and makeup, are also areas where the petite model can thrive. Additionally, in Asian markets where the samples are typically smaller, petite models are often preferred. Famous examples of petite models are Laetitia Casta (5'6), Lily-Rose Depp (5'3), Anja Konstantinova (5'4), Devon Aoki (5'5), Marilyn Monroe (5'5), Twiggy (5'6), Emily Ratajkowski (5'7), and Kate Moss (5'7).

Kate Moss was scouted at 14 years old with average height. Her agents thought she'd grow taller—she never did, but her career exploded into over two decades of fame, and she showed that height doesn't always matter.

For me, when asked my height, I always ask what it's for. I measure 5'7.5, which is neither here nor there. For acting 5'7 works, but for modeling, I'll stretch it to 5'8. After my dance years where I was never quite tall enough to be a Rockette, and too tall for hip hop, it's nice to know that my height isn't a roadblock to success in the commercial modeling arena.

Another fun fact for the petites out there is that airline companies and furniture manufacturers frequently use smaller models in their advertising campaign, so everything from a cramped airplane seat to a narrow sofa looks larger and more spacious. It's all about the proportion between the object and the talent used in the ad.

When I worked with Samsung, the kitchen appliances needed to look large and upscale. A lot of time went into arranging the shot so the talent would look small in relation to the products being photographed. The whole shoot, I wore flats and crouched in awkward angles to shrink myself.

—MATURE MODELS—

As the baby boomer generation ages, the demand for fashionable, high-quality clothing lines is in greater demand. Until now, there wasn't enough attention paid to the fit, mature figure. Most savvy markets know that people respond best to advertisements and images that reflect their specific target audience. Models over 40 are usually classified as mature, and those aged 60 and up as senior. Don't let age fool you; there's a high demand for these men and women in catalogs, insurance, financial, cruise lines, pharmaceutical, and beauty products. Most of the work for mature women is what's called "lifestyle," and it's geared specifically toward the target buying audience. Having said that, more and more, you see advertising companies request that the talent be affiliated with the product – a real Geico customer, an actual arthritis sufferer, someone with diabetes. They need the disclaimer at the bottom to ring true.

There are many successful mature models. Perhaps my favorite and most prolific one is Carmen Dell'Orefice, who has been working for more than 70 years, making her a living legend. She was born in America in 1931 but came from Italian and Hungarian lineage, and while she grew up to be a striking beauty, in an interview she gave a few years ago, Carmen was not beautiful in her mother's eyes. Her mom thought she had large ears and big feet, and at 13, she had her first photoshoot when a photographer approached her. The pictures didn't come out very well; he told her mom, "Carmen is a charming child, but she's just not photogenic at this time." Sound familiar?

Words are so powerful. Those little things people say made her feel like a failure, but at the age of 15, She was again approached by Vogue Magazine, and Carmen became the youngest Vogue Cover Girl in history.

It takes years for many models to get their break but for Carmen, it quickly catapulted her into the industry, and she started to make sixty dollars a week before she hit 18, which helped her mother transition from a starving artist to a comfortable lifestyle.

While her physical outer beauty was obviously present, her personal life was nothing like a walk in the park. She has been married three times and had lots of ups and downs facing financial difficulties throughout her career.

But at the age of 47, significantly older than her peers, with no hope or sympathy from the industry, it was running into Norman Parkinson—the famous photographer and a friend of Carmen's, that gave her the second wind to what became the beginning of her long-enduring career. She said he told her, "For an old bag, you don't look so bad."

So, they decided to team up and take a series of photos flaunting her unique ivory hair and age.

It was the beginning of the renaissance of her career. The controversial shots hit lots of publicity, Spokesperson and modeling contract opportunities started to knock on her door. Her hair became an iconic trend in the fashion world, and at 50 years old, she was again on-fire. She is now 88 years old and still busy as could be. Dell'Orefice told the Daily Mail in a 2013 interview, "I've had more covers in the past 15 years than I had in all the years before that".

Same goes for Canadian models Dayle Haddon, 71, Maye Musk, 71, French Yazemeenah Rossi, 64, and the sensational, American fashion's oldest living Icon, Iris Apfel, 98. *Geriatric Starlet* is the name she gave herself after being the subject of an exhibit at the costume institute in the Metropolitan Museum of art. These are just a few examples of successful iconic mature models demonstrating that ageless beauty doesn't have an expiration date.

—KIDS MODELING—

Could your child be a model? Most likely, yes. Agents and advertisers don't necessarily go for the most gorgeous children, and there aren't size requirements because youngsters are constantly growing and changing. This lack of rigid standards means there's a large pool of candidates for these jobs – the competition is fierce. The age groups are according to development, as follows:

- Newborn: 0-4 weeks
- Infant: 4 weeks-1 year
- Toddler: 1-3 years
- Preschooler: 4-6 years
- Child: 6-13 years
- Adolescent: 13-19 years

Finding an agent and castings are the same as with adult modeling. However, there's no need to spend money on professional images because, by the time you'll go on the next casting, your child could have grown 2 inches or lost a tooth. Clean, current, straight on images are necessary to accurately portray your child—no family members or chocolate cake in the profile images, please! It might be cute to you but distracting for agents trying to pitch the next Disney kid. Besides, there is always an additional request for social media links and digitals where the images are a lot more forgiving, and that family interaction is what the client wants to see.

Kid's modeling is as much about the parents' ability to manage their career as it is about little Johnny's cute freckles or Suzy's curls. But don't make your child live your dreams! If they are no longer interested in modeling, then be smart and don't force them into castings and bookings. Remember, too, the inevitable rejections can affect their self-esteem and psychological development from early on, just as booking a great job can boost it. The law protects minors when it comes to working on a job. You will be required to apply for a child performer permit with the Department of Labor. Every state has its own set of rules. It's mandatory for all child performers under 18 years old to get a work permit in New York State and California. It will be your responsibility as a parent or guardian to keep the permit up-to-date before any booking. Then, you'll be required to open a Coogan minor blocked trust account—15% of their gross earnings are set-aside until your child turns 18. Thanks to the Coogan Act (1999)—named for Jackie Coogan—child performers are protected from losing their earnings due to an irresponsible guardian. If your child is listed as a dependent, you will need to report their earned income to the IRS if it exceeds $12,200 in the calendar year. Thus a child can earn up to that amount without paying income tax.

And then there are child modeling scams. You've probably heard of "mall scouts" that will fawn over your child's cuteness and offer to launch their career if you pay a small fortune upfront. Like adult modeling, the only fees you should be asked to pay are, perhaps, a page on the agency's website and current images if you weren't able to take them yourself.

The career track of actress, model, and former child star Brooke Christa Shields is a prime example of the good and bad in child modeling. From controversial roles in modeling and acting to her mother acting as manager, her career was groundbreaking not just because of her skyrocketing success but because of the way the mother-daughter team took on the industry.

Brooke had her first modeling job for Ivory soap at the young age of 11 months, shot by famous photographer Francesco Scavullo. There were other modeling jobs—like being the youngest person to be in *Vogue*—throughout her youth, but it was an ad for *Calvin Klein* jeans that Brooke starred in at just 15 years old. She shot to fame not just for her looks but because of the controversy surrounding her provocative pose and the tag line; "You know what comes between me and my *Calvins*? Nothing." Many felt this was indecent.,Indecent or not, her day rate at the age of 15 was $10,000.

That controversial path continued when Brooke broke into the film industry with roles in *Pretty Baby*, where she played a child prostitute and *The Blue Lagoon*, which also had critics shouting about child pornography— despite Brooke's use of a body double.

Throughout her career, Brooke's mom guided the star's way and served as manager – or "momager" – to the young phenom. There's little doubt her business savvy served Brooke well, to the point where *Eileen Ford* actually started a children's division solely based off of Brooke's success.

The momager role is becoming more and more prevalent—look at Kris Jenner taking her Kardashian family to reality fame, Dina Lohan responsible for Lindsay's early stardom, and Miley Cyrus's career navigated by her parents. But the price paid should not be ignored. In many cases, the mother/daughter or mother/son relationship can become frayed when they have differences about the career track. It's always wise to listen to your child and not discount their opinion, no matter how young.

—YOLANDA PEREZ—

Family Model Interview

Q: *When did you start modeling, and what inspired you to start?*
A: I guess that my first introduction to the world of modeling was through a cousin of mine who took me along to one of her castings and voila! I got the job. It was an editorial spread for a Latina magazine. I was a sophomore in high school. After that, my interest in the modeling world was piqued, and I began the grueling task of searching for an agency to represent

me starting at the top of the list by attending open calls, but with no luck.

Realizing that becoming an overnight success was not in my cards, I proceeded to get a real job. I began working at a small boutique on the Upper East Side after school.

On my way to work, I would walk through Bloomingdales, hoping to be discovered there as I had read; that was where Brooke Shields was discovered, and she was my idol. As luck would have it, I was never discovered there but rather in the very store where I was working. A photographer who lived in the area asked to take my pictures and then submitted them to Click modeling agency, which was to represent me for quite a few years.

Q: What did your first portfolio contain? How many test-shoots versus editorial and ad campaigns were included?

A: Click was known for discovering new faces, so an actual portfolio was not as important as a referral from your agent.

Q: How many people in your family model and what advice do you have for aspiring models?

A: This paved the path for years of travels, photoshoots, and eventually meeting the man of my dreams who is also a model. Together we traveled quite a bit until settling down to raise three amazing daughters.

Naturally, they began the course of modeling as there was a demand for real families to portray fictional families in advertising. They are now 22, 18, and 15, and all are still active in modeling and acting.

Q: You're also a commercial/print photographer; how has that helped your modeling career? What age range are you currently covering?

A: My husband and I have progressed to a full-time photography career and still dabble in commercial print modeling in the 40-50 age group.

Q: Name three of your most exciting jobs and share what sets them apart?

A: I think that working with my family, *Osh-Kosh, Verizon, Club Med, Royal Caribbe*an, and *Motherwear Catalogue*, were some of our best jobs as we were able to go to work, travel, and spend time together.

Q: You've had a successful career that's spanned decades. Describe how the profession has influenced your lifestyle and family dynamic over the years? What role does fitness and diet play in your life?

A. Balancing family and work and a healthy lifestyle comes pretty naturally when you are all in it together.

—PARTS MODELS—

From a hand job to getting-your-foot-in-the-door, parts modeling can be particularly lucrative if you have a few specific, flawless features. Even if your face isn't the most camera-friendly or height is an issue, your long thin fingers, round perky butt, or pouched stomach could have you landing a steady stream of bookings. The following are common body parts used in such modeling:

Hands, Feet, Legs, Belly, Butt, Lips, Eyes, Neck, Back, Nose, Arms, Shoulders, Breasts, Teeth.

I recently worked with Coolsculpting, a non-surgical fat reduction technology, and though I didn't have to go for the treatment because the project was for the consumer ad, I found it interesting when I heard it was my chin and sharp angles that got me booked. I wasn't even aware that this was their focus during the casting, so it goes to show, you never know what special feature will get you booked. I've done parts modeling for years, and now, in my forties, a new asset has been discovered.

A few famous parts models—that you've probably never heard of—are Adele Uddo, Ellen Sirot, and Trisha Webster. Adele's symmetrical hands have earned her a small fortune and have been seen by millions in the *Christian Louboutin* nail polish ads. Her digits have even doubled for Penelope Cruz and Natalie Portman.

Trisha Webster's features have doubled for Gina Davis's feet, Christie Brinkley's hands, and even Susan Sarandon's legs. Her body parts are insured for a half-million dollars, and she regularly rakes in six figures.

These models protect their assets and, at times, even insure them. They most likely restrict themselves from anything that could damage their lucrative parts – hand models may not wash the dishes and could be seen wearing gloves even on a summer day. Ellen Sirot is famous for this – she has over 500 pairs of gloves to protect her moneymakers.

Just like George Costanza becoming a hand model on the Seinfeld episode 066 season 5, which is easily demonstrate how his life altered in a matter of seconds once he realized he is gifted (see QR)

Parts models are most commonly used for a variety of advertisements. All the latest tech developments are like a gold rush for hand models: holding phones, typing on a computer, and swiping at a smartphone or iPad all require hands. Jewelry, fitness apparel, food products, perfume, nail polish, lipstick, shoes, and makeup are other lucrative areas.

The pay for parts modeling—even though the talent is unrecognizable—is sometimes the same for work where the model is recognizable.

—ADELE UDDO—

Parts Model Interview

Q: When did you start modeling? What made you see parts modeling as a career opportunity?

A: I started modeling at 24, after a psychic lady, who my mother suggested I see, told me I should be a model. I tried arguing that I was too short, but she was persistent and eventually convinced me to seek out a modeling agency in San Francisco. My hunch was correct that booking jobs at my height (5'6") would be challenging. I didn't fit the sample sizes. Everything fitted for catalog, fell off me. Occasionally, I'd get beauty gigs or something commercial, but forget fashion – I was way too tiny.

Shortly after I moved to LA, my agent called one day and asked if I had nice hands. I told him my grandma seemed to think so – over the years, and more than once, she had told me I should be a hand model. But as a kid, I continued to crack my knuckles rebelliously. It turns out the casting was for OPI, and immediately I recognized a different reaction than I was used to getting at other auditions. As soon as I presented my hands, people began making little knowing nods amongst themselves, and passing my hands around the boardroom, examining them from every angle. I booked the campaign and made a card from the pictures shot, which helped me to begin booking more handwork. Maybe grandmother knows best, after all. Height isn't an issue for parts modeling. Most parts models I know are not tall model types. The industry prefers shorter girls.

Q: Which of your features are most in-demand? Which parts are you known for in the industry today?

A: My hands are definitely my most employed part. They're also the most employable since there's simply more jobs that call for hands than any other part. I also do a fair amount of lips and legs, but hands are the prized part of the industry.

Q: What types of campaigns have you worked on? Any favorites?

A: In the industry, the term "fashion hands" refers to an elegant hand – the hands you find on jewelry or cosmetics campaigns, or in fashion magazines, for instance. Whereas a "commercial hand" fits into the category of every day—the hand-next-door you'd see on a Clorox commercial. I'm primarily known as a high-end hand, but I do a lot of commercials as well. Often, it comes down to nail length and polish color – hands can look dramatically different with a little length and color. For the most part, I book beauty or luxury brands: Dior, Revlon, Juicy, Christian Louboutin, etc. I've been lucky to represent some amazing companies and work with the best people in the biz, so it's hard to pick a favorite. It's always exciting when a celebrity is on set. My hands were blushing a bit when I worked with Colin Farrell. And I've always been a big fan of Beyoncé, so when I worked with her on a *L'Oreal* commercial, I tried acting cool, but inside I was super starstruck. I love *Christian Louboutin*, so launching his polish line was exciting. I also work regularly with Essie, and always have fun with that team. And I love Deborah Lippmann, so when I did her lipstick campaign, that was quite a thrill. I can't pick a favorite.

Q: You mentioned earlier that parts modeling is one of the few careers where you can be featured on billboards yet remain unrecognizable. How do you feel about it? Do you prefer that anonymity?

A: You're right, I'm usually unrecognizable in the final image. It's been convenient that my career allows me to hide behind my hands (so to speak) since I can be a pretty private person. There's always been a part of me that wants to be seen, and another side that wants to remain hidden, so the anonymity of parts modeling is kind of perfect for me.

Q: Do part modeling images pay different rates than mainstream modeling images?

A: Whenever you're unrecognizable, the rates are a lot lower. It's unfortunately rare to get big buyouts when your face isn't shown. No matter how big the campaign, if it's parts only, you're making a fraction of what a principle model makes on the same job. That's, in part, why the parts biz got popular; clients didn't want to pay top models top dollar to shoot their limbs. I've also heard from models who worked in the '80s, and 90's that the rates are not as good as they used to be back then. Unfortunately, inflation has continued to rise while pay-for-print has gone down.

Q: What do you get more of, part print modeling work or part acting in film & commercial?

A: It wasn't until I became bicoastal and began working in New York, that my career took off. The bulk of beauty and fashion is focused in NYC, so parts modeling is really big on the East Coast, particularly print. L.A. is more of a commercial town. There's a big glamour gap between the two coasts – one day, I'll be in New York, shooting cosmetics for Dior, and the next day I'll be in L.A., promoting chicken parts for El Pollo Loco.

Q: What is the criteria for good hands, legs, feet, lips, chin, etc.? Are different models getting known specifically for their various parts, like typecasting in the acting world?

A: Beauty is so subjective. What one client wants may have nothing to do with what the next client perceives as beautiful. Typically, a fashion hand has long skinny fingers, thinner wrists, whereas a commercial hand is a little less specific, just nice nail beds and a healthy-looking hand. Like many businesses, you get known for something you do well and get rehired on similar jobs as your resume grows. In my case, I tend to book beauty most often, which is great since it's what I most enjoy shooting.

Q: What is your beauty regimen to keep up your beautiful, healthy, and radiant skin?

A: My motto is to MOISTURIZE. I'm a strong believer that a little lotion goes a long way. That's primarily how I take care of my skin and prepare my parts for jobs. Moisture makes skin and hands look healthy. For years I've been making my own moisturizers from coconut oil, shea butter, sweet almond oil, and a blend of essential oils that are great for the skin. I'm currently formulating a lotion for face, and all parts, made from my favorite natural ingredients. I also believe eating healthy contributes to how I look and feel. I'm not one of those models who claim to eat cake and a bowl of bacon grease for breakfast.

Q: In a world of so much computer-generated images and Photoshop programs, can you still lose a job over a broken nail, blister, tattoo, or tan lines? If so, do you feel that you'd rather lay low on adventures prior to an upcoming casting or shoot?

A: Besides being a bit obsessive about applying lotion, I'm not crazy careful with my hands. I've learned to slow down my movements and be more mindful, so I don't show up to a job with bruised chins or broken nails. Sure, you're allowed to be human (thank God), so a bruise or zit is forgivable. I've had my share of both, and Photoshop can usually take care of those things. Unless a company is looking for someone with tattoos, they rarely want to spend the money or take the time in post-production to remove something, when they could simply cast someone without tattoos in the first place.

Q: Name 3 of your most exciting jobs, what sets them apart?

A: In a previous question, I talked about some favorite clients/jobs. I think what makes the best job is a combo of the team you're working with, the skill level of everyone involved, and the brand you're representing. It's exciting to see great artists work, whether a photographer, makeup artist, nail tech, stylist, etc. Sometimes it's the brand you're shooting – Dior is one of my favorite designers, so it's always exciting to be part of anything they do. A great location can also contribute to how cool a job is – I did the last Bellagio campaign, and it was fun spending a couple of nights in Vegas. Also, don't underestimate the contribution of great craft service and catering – good food can certainly impact the mood on any set.

—JIM FORSHA—

All-American, Mature/Hand Model Interview

Q: When did you start modeling? What inspired you to get started?

A: Interestingly, I started while I was in the midst of another career as a teacher. I taught high school and college level English for nine years full-time. Someone around that time said, "You ought to be using that face— you could make some money." Having mentioned that to my sister, she, unbeknownst to me, sent a photo of me to a local model agency and they called me in for an interview; the rest, as they say, is history.

Q: What did your first portfolio contain, and how many test shoots versus editorial or ad campaigns were included?

A: You have to realize that I started out in "the boonies" of Pennsylvania. So my first shoot(s)/portfolio were very limited. That portfolio included two photoshoots (one general and one done in Philadelphia, which concentrated more on a fashion/editorial look) and any and all tear sheets I'd begun to acquire.

Q: How many agencies are you currently with, and how often do you do test shoots to provide current images?

A: At one point, I counted and listed everyone who called me for modeling work—agents, casting agents, producers, etc. I came up with 41. I know, sounds crazy, but I found that I wasn't that guy who could book enough work through just one agent, so I caught on with whomever I could, figuring that, hopefully, if others weren't calling, at least one or two might be!

Q: What advice do you have for aspiring models entering the fashion world at a younger age?

A: Make sure it's something you want to do, something you enjoy doing. Don't do it for the money. Please don't do it because others want you to. Try it; see if you like it, and if so, throw yourself into it!

Q: You are considered the "All-American" type. How has your look/background helped you conquer your market? What age range do you go for?

A: Well, I've been doing this now for over 30 years (yeesh!), so things have evolved many times. Unfortunately for me, the good old "All-American" look that used to be so in demand is not only no longer in vogue, but has been replaced by our culture's changing melting pot of ethnicities— and I don't think there's any going back. Still, one is "stuck" with his look, and if you keep an eye on what's current, you have to adjust. As my age range has climbed (I'm not doing 48 – 56), I've gone from doing "young couples"/parents to corporate and businessman to older parents, etc. Lately, I've been doing a lot of pharmaceuticals, which have become huge. I'm lucky that I'm somehow the age, the "type" (to play a doctor often), and that the epicenter of the pharmaceutical industry seems to be in the Northeastern US, where I'm located. It doesn't hurt that the pharmaceutical companies have very large advertising budgets and pay their models well!

Q: Name three of your most exciting jobs/accounts, and what sets them apart?

A: Whoa, that's a tough one. The one that people most like to hear about is when I doubled for Robert De Niro in "Meet the Parents." I went into the audition as a hand model, but they liked me so much—particularly how meticulously I followed his original moves, that they used me for all of De Niro's close-ups (which he couldn't do because he had to move forward with all of the other master scenes). There are hundreds of others of note—getting to kiss Nicole Kidman in a film, making $7500 for less than two hours playing a father lifting his 10-year-old daughter who runs to meet him; even recently not only NOT having to pay for injections to eliminate facial wrinkles, but being paid A LOT to have it done (and doing "before and after" photos, as well as interviews about the process). Just start mentioning different kinds of modeling work, and I can list dozens more.

Q: You've had a successful career that allowed you excessive traveling, Describe how this profession has influenced your lifestyle and choices over the years?

A: Well, for good or for bad? I will never be able to go back to a "real job"—stuck in the same place every day and doing essentially the same thing. The absolute best thing about my job: Something different and interesting every day, great places, intriguing people, things the average person doesn't get to see or do. I have a friend who tells me I should get a "real job"—for security and certainty. My response, "When you have to go to work, you say, 'Oh, I have to work tomorrow. I hate it.' When I get called for work, I say, 'Yahoo, I get to work.' I'm ecstatic!" Also, I find that I have much more free time than most people—which is huge for me. Finally, if there's ever a job I don't want to do—and I'm not in need of a paycheck—I say I'm not available. Sometimes nice weather calls me to the golf course instead of the photo studio—most people can't make that decision. I don't plan on being one of those people who, at life's end, says his greatest regret is "Working too much" (which is what a recent survey revealed).

Q: What role does fitness and diet play in your life, any secrets to share?

A: I wish I were more adamant about a good diet and fitness program. I am lucky, not only genetically speaking, but in that, I was always an athlete and interested in working out. That's the only thing that allows me to eat all those sweets that I feel also genetically programmed to "need." I can't NOT work out more than a day or two.

Q: As a commercial model with several agencies, how important is it to keep track of all your bookkeeping, submissions, and material updates? Is it fair to say that you're always in the driver's seat?

A: Again, I'm lucky—I've always been an organized person, especially regarding finances and such. But I must say: This is of utmost importance if one is going to work in this business. No one else is going to watch these things for you (including your taxes, health care, retirement accounts, etc.). Since these things are so "nebulous" in that you're not working a "normal job" and have lots of different people supposed to be paying you—things can not only get confusing, but there are those factions out there who will try to take advantage of you and your situation. Keep an eye on it all; don't let yourself be a victim.

—BODY DOUBLE & PHOTO DOUBLE—

As mentioned in parts, a double could be someone who is used to stand-in for the principal cast member, star, or celebrity. The double will resemble the cast member in height, size, measurements, and skin tone to seamlessly create the illusion that it's the same actor on-screen at all times. Photo & body doubles can be used in commercials and movies as well as print.

Doubles are typically requested in scenarios where an actor doesn't feel comfortable with nudity, sexual situations, or a stunt scene. They're also used if the principal talent or actor wishes to have someone with better features in their place, for instance, wrinkle-free hands, a cellulite-free butt, or simply a bigger better chest. One example would be the late Paul Walker, the lead star in the "Fast and Furious" franchise, who died while the seventh installment was still, in production, his look-alike brother stepped in to finish the scenes featuring Paul. The replacement ensured continuity despite the loss of the film's main actor. Even some of the most adventurous celebrities may choose not to reveal all. In the film "Wanted," Angeline Jolie opted for a body double rather than go au-natural herself for the nude scene. But by the same token, when it comes to stunts, she does 99% of her own, including the fight scenes in Salt and aerial stunts in Maleficent. Jackie Chan is also notorious for doing his own stunts. Not only fight scenes but everything from jumping out of hot air balloons to explosion scenes—you name it, he's done it, and Hollywood loves it. That said, most actors prefer to leave the dirty work to professionals.

CHAPTER THREE

—ON CAMERA—

W hether you're an aspiring thespian or not, you may consider getting a commercial agent to send you out for on-camera auditions.
These jobs include:

—BROADCAST MEDIA (TV/RADIO/NEW MEDIA)—

Television Commercials are the largest and most expensive medium to advertise. You have the advantage of being able to creatively express the brand message to a wide audience in a short amount of time. With the advent of DVR and the mute button, many potential consumers go unreached, seeing the commercials as a distraction to their programming.

Radio is another medium that reaches a vast audience spectrum, allowing a few fleeting moments for you to pitch your brand or product message. Compared to television, it's a more affordable means of advertising. While many assume radio is dead, research shows that's not the case. According to Nielsen's Media Research data published by the radio advertising bureau in 2019, 272 million Americans listen to traditional radio every week. The audience for terrestrial radio remains steady and high, suggesting 89% of Americans over the age of 12 tuned in weekly. Back in the day, I used to love driving my son to school and texting my friend Ian O'Malley, a DJ on a New York station Q 104.3, who would kindly congratulate my son on his various successes. Even if you don't have a direct line to a DJ, the radio is a great way to connect and send messages rather than having earbuds in all the time.

New Media is a phrase that describes mass communication through digital technologies using the internet and its infinite apps, which are now the #1 go-to advertising platform to promote products and services. Banner ads and pop-ups are a constant for Internet users, and they are tailored based on your search habits. These examples are just the icing on the cake. New media, from webisodes to webinars, these online platforms are constantly developing and growing in popularity. At the time of publication, SAG/AFTRA was still ironing out agreements for these various platforms, though acknowledges that the situation is fluid.

There are different types of advertising and a client should consider what approach to use. **Brand Advertising** is used by prominent companies with substantial budgets hoping to differentiate their brand and build a long term following. Relationship building advertising may offer free samples or promotions and discounts. **Direct Sales** is another avenue, all those annoying infomercials asking you to call in and buy their product now.

As you can see, there are many ways to present a commercial. Clients will use different tactics to deliver their message. Here are some common methods:

Infomercials: these commercials will normally be longer spots and much more informative.

Testimonials: the talent discusses their experience and satisfaction with a specific product or service.

Associations/Celebrity/Influencers: Association and using a celebrity for branding is another way to captivate an audience. This tactic is frequently used with food, fragrances, Jewelry, automotive fashion, and more. The strategy behind celebrity association is that the audience trusts the opinion of these icons and wants to imitate their lifestyle. This makes me think of one of my favorite movies, The Joneses (2009), written and directed by Derrick Borte. It's a "social commentary on our consumerist society," using product placement and branding as the driving force behind the plot. The Joneses are the picture-perfect family living the American dream, with their consumer goods always on-display for their neighbors to covet. What the neighbors don't know is it's all a farce; they're paid to be a living advertisement-stealth marketing at its best. Other single candidates of celebrity endorsements examples are Sophia Vergara for *Pepsi*, George Clooney for *Nespresso*, Jennifer Aniston for *Smart Water*, Jennifer Garner for *Capital One*, and the list goes on.

For companies with a large budget, a great way to build trust and brand awareness is to create a series of commercials using the same "star." Think of the *Geico* gecko character played by Jake Wood, or Flo for *Progressive Auto Insurance* – played by Stephanie Courtney whose been named one of the top female commercial icons of our time. After more than a decade of auditions and small roles, she landed her big break with Progressive shooting over 100 commercials for the corporation since 2008 and earning nearly a million dollars per year for her advertisements.

Same goes for the famous Super Bowl warrior commercial featuring Jason Momoa for *Rocket Mortgage*, or the creation of "Can you hear me now" by Paul Marcarelli for *Verizon*, where, as a stage actor, he just signed a small contract to be the "test man," one that led to a 10 million dollar endorsement 10 years later. Appealing to consumer's vanity, these types of advertisements are mostly very

visual and light on dialogue. These ads use the opposite gender and great cinematic visuals to entice the consumer.

—HOSTING—

For a long time, actors shied away from hosting, fearing it would take them out of contention for legit work. But now hosting has become popular, with many actors gaining celebrity status for their work. Hosting gigs can be scripted or non-scripted, improvised, or sketched. Successful hosts are quick-on-their-feet, witty, approachable yet well-spoken and articulate. A sense of humor and authenticity are key elements along with the ability to connect with the camera, live audience, or your interviewees. Hosting is not the same as acting because you are playing your most confident self. You're also most likely using a teleprompter or memorizing a lengthy monologue, rather than reacting to a fellow actor.

Yet, hosting traits are ones that actors naturally possess. Excellent projection, fearlessness, advanced skills, and self-focusing. If that's the direction you are considering, practice lines in front of the mirror, work on pronunciations, and deliver them as yourself and not as a character would.

Regis Philbin started his career hosting talk shows. His unique Bronx accent and irreverent ad-libs set him apart from the others. Nick Cannon is another example of someone who rose to fame as a host of America's Got Talent. Mario Lopez, initially famous for his role as Slater on Saved By The Bell, traded in acting for hosting and hasn't looked back since. Kelly Ripa began her acting career on All My Children and now boasts one of the top hosting Emmy winning jobs of all time starting at, Live with Regis and Kelly 2001-2011, to now, Live with Kelly and Ryan, but the second seat has been dynamically shifting through the years.

Chris Harrison, the host of many shows, including The Bachelor, The Bachelorette, and Who Wants to Be a Millionaire, is an example of a successful on-air talent who has strictly been a host, starting as a sports reporter and moving on to the major networks.

Often, actors are surprised to find their true niche is to be a host, playing themselves. For others, it's an added means of exposure to enhance their acting career.

Hosting is not just for actors, but models as well. QVC and the Home Shopping Network use models as spokespeople. These often become lucrative and steady jobs for models.

—VOICEOVERS—

Do people compliment you on your Golden Tongue? If so, you may consider pursuing work as a voiceover talent.

There are plenty of recording studios eager to put your voice on file in their extensive sound bite libraries. But before you can start booking work, you'll need to make a demo reel, which can consist of radio or TV copy as a starter. Making the audio demo reel is the equivalent of a showreel for actors and composite card for models. This won't cost as much as a reel or comp card and may get you work right away – even if you're inexperienced. More so than experience, it's your voice that determines whether you get the part, though as you book voiceover roles, be sure to include that on your resume – clients always like booking professionals with experience.

To create your voiceover demo reel, get a mic, find some copy, start practicing breathing, and reading properly. If you speak multiple languages, be sure to include examples of you speaking in each one, as this significantly expands your pool of potential clients.

If you're stuck or unsure of where to start, there are many classes at recording studios that offer these services. Some different class types include character and animation technique, accent and intonation, public speaking, and hosting, among others.

Let's recap the steps: Find classes – record demo reel – find an agent – audition – book a job – repeat – build a resume.

The key to working successfully at the professional level is the number of seconds it takes you to deliver certain phrases. This, of course, takes practice, but that's one of the things the producers are looking for when casting new voiceover talent. You also want to consider that this work can be very repetitive, and you'll find yourself standing on your feet in the booth repeating scripts in different intonation, so immerse yourself, get creative, and have fun with the possibilities and see where your imagination takes you.

The voiceover industry has many types of voices that are considered to be great assets but, when hearing them in every-day conversations, you may not think they would be in high demand. For example, heavy smokers find themselves desirable for voiceover work as the harsh, low, and sultry sound works wonders for certain clients. The same goes for high-pitched, quirky voices. Accents and languages are also in high demand in the voiceover industry. If you have the triple-threat effect in that field (good voice, variety of accents, several languages), you should consider voiceover as a career option.

The following are key elements in determining your vocal characteristics:

1. Categorize your vocal type: soprano, mezzo-soprano, contralto, tenor, baritone, bass, or one of the many grey areas in between.
2. Age range: This determines the notes your body can produce.
3. Physical characteristics: Size and weight determine the amount of sound you can produce and whether it's light, bright, heavy, rich, dark, powerful, (does it sound like I'm describing a cup of coffee or

glass of wine?).
4. Speaking range and the point where you move from chest to head register.

Keep in mind a teen's voice isn't final until they reach 25; this is especially true for men. When you try to classify the voice of someone younger, expect it to change dramatically until their mid-twenties. Don't rush to typecast their voice.

Your most profitable genres in voiceover will typically align with your natural assets. The natural voice should be the first thing placed on your reel. Think of it – if you emphasize too much artificial dialect or accents that aren't natural to you might miss the market. It's great if you can do a southern accent, but in reality, they'll probably book someone with an actual southern accent. Often your natural voice is just what they are looking for. I can personally confess that when I came to America, I worked hard to eliminate my Israeli accent and not be the foreigner that I was since ethnic talent wasn't a hot market as it is now. Years later, with the creation of Gal Gadot playing Wonder Woman, that Israeli accent is in high demand. Luckily, I can still hear my mom speaking English to her housekeeper, who is from South Africa, in her thick Israeli accent, and time stands still. It comes right back to me.

Look into what jobs are common in your market. In big cities, you might find more cartoon voice work, live demonstrations, corporate narrations, and promos than in smaller markets. But it's most essential to enjoy the genre you choose whether it's working with kids, doing narration for documentary, or doing commercials.

Voiceover is a business like any other business. Rarely will you be discovered from a spot you did, as is the case with parts modeling. But, with time, you'll build your credits and clientele base on your great reputation, professionalism, and work relationships. Terminology expertise and a creative personality will help you to thrive in this segment of the industry.

—INDUSTRIAL—

Industrial is usually training videos or a demo reel for a company to demonstrate their business or product. Hence, industrial = industry-based. You might find yourself teaching how to do the laundry step-by-step, how to use the curling iron, or simply show how to deposit a check at the bank. These are very common and handy gigs that are often available. You get a payday rate with no residuals, but most of the time, it's minimal exposure for the talent. These gigs are great "day jobs" and hey, you're in front of the camera!

—LIVE DEMONSTRATION/LIVE EXPO—

Live demonstration is, as it sounds, showing how something is done. Many companies choose to gather their clients and make a live demonstration with actors to display their new line of products, work services, etc. It's quite common in many industries, from hair products, fitness products, and computer software. The gigs are normally a few hours, and you'll only get paid for your time that day since it's live no residuals apply. The good news is these are often done multiple days in a row at expo centers/market exhibits across the country. For example, when I worked for Canon on their new Cameras Expo, we had to reinforce a scene that was played repetitively while the cameras streamed. In those moments, it showed how the camera was able to capture specific details of the sets and actions while our host explained the product features and new gimmicks. It required preparation to memorize the script and camera features and functions, but nothing different from preparing for a theater scene to be replayed.

—INTERACTIVE (MOTION CAPTURE/VIDEO GAMES)—

Motion capture uses special technology and sensors to record the actions of actors or dancers to animate characters in computer animation. Superhero movies are a prime example of the use of motion capture, as is the character Gollum from Lord of the Rings. When I worked for *Rockstar* and other videogame or animation companies, whether it was a dance scene, a combat sequence, or playing another active scenario, it was all done using CGI technology. My job was to dress in super tight head-to-toe suits covered with sensor balls called markers, and do the requested actions. In my case, it was to compose the choreography with my partner and portray the main actor in this most famous game series, you got it, *Grand Theft Auto*. Such information is captured by the computer and used in the animation programming. It was quite amazing to witness every move I took being transposed to the on-screen character in real-time.

These video games are so realistic, thanks to this technology, that they are more like interactive movies, the experience elaborate, and cinematic. Even though it wasn't reflecting my identified image on screen, the experience working behind the scenes on this animation was extremely gratifying.

For a while, the terms of employment for Motion Capture Actors were up for debate, but after much negotiation, it's been determined that performance motion capture is subject to the usual on-camera rate.

—INFOMERCIAL—

Information commercial. These can be done on T.V., radio, or web. It's a long spot of advertisement with information on a product: how to use it, why to use it, and how to buy it, NOW! Most of the time, it uses several unique techniques such as testimonial—people talking about their experience using the product. Infomercials also use time pressure techniques such as, "the price is only good for the next twenty minutes, so call now!" These advertisements use models to show how the product works and how it's miraculously different from any other product out there so far. They offer guarantees as insurance. These testimonials are intended to add legitimacy and a personal connection to the individual interested in purchasing the product.

Infomercial jobs are typically a day rate with no residuals. This is mostly non-union work since it goes to various cable channels.

—ANIMATION (STORYBOARD & GREEN SCREENS)—

Animation is another underestimated source of work for actors. Animation is created by a series of drawings, images, photographs, or objects that are viewed one after another, creating a movement effect. Growing up, I used to connect the use of animation, mainly with cartoons – by now, things have changed. Nowadays, with CGI, 2D, 3D, typography sand, clay, flipbook, stop motion, and green screens, the use of animation techniques are endless.

Below is a great example of a green screen shoot conducted by Photographer Matt Karas at his Karasmattik Studio in NYC with Talent (John Di Domenico and myself) image later imposed in front of the White House. Such a shoot is cost-effective and easier to achieve in a shorter time, which is the case, nine times out of ten. So you can understand the productivity of greenscreen usage and how you can save shots for a later date to be imposed over a different background.

The same goes for the Pharmaceutical shoot for *Humira*. As you can see, a studio shoot manipulated to look like a remote location shoot.

Now, getting back to animated storyboards. I want to share with you my conversation with Ezra Krausz, Founder & CEO of Animated Storyboards. In the following interview is a link to the walkthrough steps of the creation of a commercial, from the drawings of the storyboard to the final commercial, which can be viewed by scanning the QR code at the beginning of the interview.

—EZRA KRAUSZ—

Founder and CEO of Animated Storyboards Interview

Q: As the founder and CEO of Animated Storyboards, you've watched the industry evolve dramatically. What prompted you to get into this business, and how has it changed since that time?

A: In 2000, I attended a short animation course in Macromedia Flash (then a new internet software). After realizing the great potential value it may have to the pre-visual industry, and having a commercial production already, I put together some Animated Storyboard samples and started to market it with advertising agencies in NY and Chicago.

Q: How do you define an animated storyboard?

A: An Animated Storyboard is an animated short commercial movie that visualizes a script for a TV commercial. This Animated Storyboard will then be used as a testing material at focus groups to evaluate the potential effectiveness of the tested concept.

Q: What is the evolution of a storyboard? What are the steps from brainstorming to a final product?

A: The first stage is getting the job awarded: bidding, and pitching the agency to get the job. Next, the agency creative team (producer, creative director, copywriter, and art director) will brief the ASB (Animated Storyboards) team by phone or in-person meeting. The next stage will be ASB presenting sketch storyboards, characters, and backgrounds, composited colored boards, and finally animated scenes on a timeline with an accompanying soundtrack. The entire process from Award to ship will take around 2-3 weeks in total.

Q: Where do actors come into play with animated storyboards? How frequently do you use them? How important is their presence for the illustrator?

A: Actors are often used in a pre-illustration stage for real-life reference. Facial expressions that convey human emotion, body language, and action are crucial for the accuracy and success of delivering the visual message. Motion capture acting is frequently needed as well.

Q: What is the job of the actor?

A: In addition to serving as a reference for the illustrators and animators, live shoots are also part of the previsual world. Often Animated Storyboards will produce Live HD test commercial shots mostly on green screen with live-action actors.

Q: Who decides the criteria for selecting actors in animated projects?

A: ASB producers are in charge of finding and booking actors and visual talent, sometimes based on direct connections with the talent but mostly with local casting agents.

Q: Name some of your favorite projects. What sets them apart?

A: Pepsi, "Joy of Dance," a Super Bowl commercial with Janelle Monáe. This project combined art direction, periodical challenges, and different choreographed dancing, and the Denver Broncos won the Super Bowl.

Scan the code to see: The Pepsi, "Joy of Dance," Super Bowl Animated Storyboard Commercial.

—IMPERSONATORS—

An interview with John Di Domenico
Emmy Nominated, award-winning actor, writer and Impersonator

Q: Can you share a little background of how you got started in this business of impersonation? Also, when did you realize you had talent and discovered your niche?

A: When I was a kid, I lived in Ambler, Pennsylvania. The neighborhood I was in was like South Philly; it was all row homes, and everyone would sit out on their steps during the warm weather. When I was five years old, I had a severe speech impediment, but for some reason, when I did impressions, it vanished. So by doing impressions, I've made people laugh, got affirmation, and approval from adults. It was always great to make other kids laugh, but to make adults laugh was so much fun. I would watch Ed Sullivan and see some of the impersonators and impressionists on his show, and I would come out that evening and do that very same act. I was a big ham, and all I knew was, at five years old, I wanted to be an actor, comedian, entertainer.

When I entered school, they tested me, and I spent the next eight years, two times a week, working with multiple speech pathologists on my speech impediment. Over the course of that time, my impediment was corrected, and I was given the gift of learning how to change my voice through all of the sessions of speech therapy. Basically, they gave me a much better understanding of vocal production and how to manipulate my voice.

Q: How many years have you been doing it, and how many characters are you comfortable with?

I've been a comedian performer since I was five years old, so that would be over 50 years, at this point. Professionally, I started acting when I was 24, so professionally, over 30 years. I do about 30 different characters in full makeup, wardrobe, and wig; there's probably 10 of them that I am extremely adept at, including Donald Trump, Austin Powers, Dr. Evil, Dr. Phil, Larry King, Jay Leno, Guy Fieri, Chris Matthews, Regis Philbin, and Lieutenant Colombo.

Q: Would you say that this is a good alternative for people wanting to pursue acting? Also, how far is that from the mainstream, or does the work tend to merge?

This is an excellent alternative for someone pursuing acting and also very complimentary. Some of the most well-known actors are incredible impressionists and impersonators because that's what they do. If you look at Christian Bale playing Dick Cheney, or Jamie Foxx playing Ray Charles, or Meryl Streep playing Margaret Thatcher, and many more, they are impersonating that person; they are doing an impression of their voice, they are adding the emotional component of acting, but the other elements; voice, look, physicality have to be there for a believable performance.

The work merges. I've done multiple TV series' and feature films because of my ability to impersonate well-known people.

Q: You are known to be the #1 Trump impersonator in the world, can you share with me how this all came about?

A: I've always been fascinated by Trump. I grew up in the Philadelphia area and wanted to be an actor in New York City. In the 1980s, when I started to research New York as a place to live, the name that kept popping up in general, was Donald Trump. I was also working in Atlantic City in the late 80s at some of his hotel-casinos. By 1990, I was doing a show at Trump Plaza. He was a fascinating guy, and I even bought his book Art of the Deal. It was always in my universe since I worked in New York City, Atlantic City, and Philadelphia, and by the late 80s through the 90s, he was becoming a dominant figure in pop-culture in the Northeastern United States.

One of the things I've always specialized in is learning difficult voices, and in 2004, right after the first season of The Apprentice ended, I received a call from an agent—it was a Friday—asking me if I had started doing Donald Trump yet. His voice had been rolling around in my head for quite a while. It turned out it was for a voiceover project, and the audition was on Monday. I ran out that day and bought the first season of the apprentice, which had just hit the shelves, and spent 30 hours learning his voice. I went to the audition on Monday, and I booked it. It turned out to be a very large multi-day project impersonating Trump's voice.

Soon after that, another agent called and said, "I heard you're doing Trump, are you doing full wardrobe, makeup, and wig? "I said, "Not yet, but I could, if there's enough lead time"; which there was. The booking was a month away, so I went into New York City and met with Bob Kelly, who built all the wigs for Saturday Night Live and all of the Broadway shows—this was 2005. He built my wig, and then I started doing live appearances as

Trump. My first booking was for a corporate event, and then soon after that, I was hired to do a cross-promotion for the next season of the apprentice and Marriott hotels. The promotion appeared on Fox and friends, and, as far as I know, I am the first person ever to appear as Donald Trump on national television other than Darrell Hammond on Saturday Night Live. Since Trump has announced his run for the presidency, my life has changed, and I pretty much do Trump in some capacity every single day of the week; either radio, voiceovers, live appearances, Cameos, movies, TV shows, or web series'.

Q: What is your typical daily routine?

A: I am up at 6 AM. Stretch, workout, check the news, and find out what happened overnight since I live in Las Vegas, and I'm three hours behind East Coast. I then head to the office, check my workload, scripts, contracts, and do emails, billing, expenses, book travel, etc. I usually have at least one or two voiceovers, so I head into the audio studio, record those, and upload them to my clients. Then I'm in the makeup chair, and by the afternoon, I am in Trump wardrobe, and I'm shooting videos on my White House press room set into the evening. If I'm on the road shooting a series, film, or performing live at national sales meetings, I'm up very early, rehearsals, makeup, wardrobe, wig, and then I'm on set or on stage.

Q: How do you prepare for impersonating a character?

A: Usually, I break the voice down in eight elements, for example, throat placement, nasal placement, vocal production, cadence, etc., to get the impression right. I write all of that down in a notebook, along with breaking down the physicality of the person I am impersonating. I talk to my wig person, and we build a wig that looks like a person's hair. I talk to my makeup person, and we design a makeup pattern that I can replicate. I talk to my wardrobe person, and we put together the wardrobe that is either exactly the same or approximates the person I'm impersonating. Then it's just practice, practice, practice.

Q: What are the types of engagements you get?

A: My daily engagements are voiceovers for a number of different clients, including a podcast and a TV show in Australia; also, radio calls. The larger part of my day, I shoot Trump cameos and some of my other characters, usually six days a week. Cameos are two-minute videos people buy for friends as a gift. I also shoot promos for business clients, mostly as Trump.

On a weekly basis, I do national and international sales meetings around the world, and I've been lucky enough to work all over the globe as all of my different characters. Since I live in Las Vegas, I've joined the cast of a number of shows there.

When my schedule allows it, I'm able to work on TV and film projects, sometimes as myself or sometimes as characters.

Q: Can you share some of the highlights from bookings, to interviews, to special people you meet in the process?

A: I've had the opportunity to work all over the world. I shot a commercial in Israel as Jay Leno; I received an Emmy nomination for a commercial that I shot in the Boston TV market where I played six celebrity characters. People magazine did a story on my Austin Powers impersonation. I've done over 300 interviews about my Trump impersonation, including multiple articles in the New York Times, Washington Post, McClatchy newspapers, Las Vegas Review-Journal, and many more. I have appeared on the Conan O'Brien Show & Fox News over 50 times as Trump. I've appeared on TODAY in Australia 10 times, 6 times in the U.K. Number-one-rated morning show, This Morning. I got to perform as Trump at the European Parliament and the Rainbow Room at 30 Rock for a star-studded audience. I've opened for Alec Baldwin and worked on a film with Kim Kardashian. My Trump viral video has been played on Howard Stern. I've also won two different awards for my Trump Impersonation, from the Laugh Factory in Los Angeles and one from ABC's, The View, where I was considered the best in two competitions.

Q: How political do you have to get when in costume, especially doing Trump.

A: My goal is to entertain everyone. It doesn't matter what your political stripe is. I want to make you laugh, so I try not to get too political and focus more on Trump's personality and the things that he has said. There's a great deal of humor in his personality, and I'd rather focus on that and bring people together rather than divide them.

Q: Can you share the story of how you matched up with Israeli Melania and the work you are creating together?

A: A friend of mine, Matt Karas, who I had been working with for years on multiple acting projects, introduced us. He shot some great videos of me and some photos as Trump. He mentioned he knew an actress by the name of Mira Tzur, who was not only a dead ringer for Melania but prettier. He also mentioned that she had an Israeli accent that would work very well for the character. The next time I was in New York City—he and I were shooting—he invited Mira down to his studio. When I met Mira, I knew we hit it off and had a great working chemistry. She is extremely intelligent and knows the business so well. She knows what works visually because of her modeling background, but since she's a producer, she also knows what works from the production side. She is a great blend of the artistic, the creative, and the business. We took some Trump/Melania photos together, and as soon as we saw them, we knew we had lightning in a bottle. We went outside the studio and shot on the streets of New York, where I, as Trump, directed traffic with Melania/Mira on my arm, that video went viral.

Mira and I went on to become friends and collaborate on numerous

Trump/Melania live bookings and photo shoots. On one occasion, we were shooting in front of Trump international at Columbus Circle, and a South Korean TV crew thought we were Trump and Melania since there was a police presence.

NYT Article about
John Di Domenico

*Melania and Donald
Trump Body Double*

—'EXTRA' WORK—

Like stock photography for print modeling, extra work for actors can be a great way to introduce yourself to the industry. You get the experience of being on-set, often with familiar actors, and learn the technical aspect of filmmaking. The hours are long and the pay low, so use it as a learning experience or to get your SAG-AFTRA card. If you decide that you want to pursue this career seriously, make sure you are well represented with a legit agent and shift to find the right principle roles for you.

When I first started back in my early 20's, I booked a few featured-extra roles in popular films and television. Fortunately, when on set, I was bumped into a principal contract and given a few lines. Even though some of those scenes ended up on the cutting room floor, I still receive the residual checks to this day.

As a non-union talent, once you book a job, you'll have a payday, and that will usually be it. If you're Union, you'll receive a day rate based on your SAG-AFTRA or other union affiliations guidelines, but the residuals will continue as long as the spot or show runs.

—UNIONS: TO JOIN OR NOT TO JOIN—

Whether you're a trained actor or model interested in booking national commercials, this is a question you will inevitably face and one that's not always easy to answer. There are many pros and cons to joining a union, and considerable thought should be given to how these can impact your future career.

The Pros: Unions, especially SAG-AFTRA—the largest film and television union—have considerable power when negotiating wages for their actors. Wage negotiations cover everything from the base day rate, called "scale," to upgrades in pay for special skills and stunts. In this chart (scan the QR below) you can see television and commercial union rate sheet for 2019 and the various ways the union has negotiated on behalf of their talent; meal penalties, overtime, travel expenses, smoke, hazards, and a variety of others instances can bump up your pay rate dramatically.

When you work on a union job, you might be booked as an extra, stunt, or body double, and end up bumped to a principal contract. A prime example of this is when Matthew McConaughey booked his first film, Dazed and Confused. It was supposed to be a three-day job, but the director liked him so much it turned into a three-week role that earned him a SAG card and lifetime of residuals. This also applies in the commercial world when you get an upgrade contract to principal; you'll receive residuals as long as the spot runs.

Residuals are another major benefit to working as a union talent. Once you have a contract signed as a principal actor, you're entitled to residuals each time that episode or film airs for the rest of your life – even if you ended up on the cutting room floor!

Unions also set the rules for working conditions and have representatives that keep an eye on production to ensure those standards are met. Union actors are generally seen as more serious as it takes significant effort to become eligible and to keep your union dues and statues intact, though some would say that such stereotype is changing with the rise of independent filmmaking.

Some unions, including SAG-AFTRA, also offer health insurance coverage and retirement plans if your income from acting meets a certain threshold.

The Cons: There is less work available for union actors. Increasing numbers of productions are choosing to remain non-union to avoid the hassle and expense of meeting union standards. That said, non-union films and commercials can be great resume builders and stepping-stones to a successful career and shouldn't be considered inferior.

Unions can come into play even where you'd least expect. I've missed several opportunities to work with advertising agencies that wanted to use my images for print. When they found out I'm a union member, they knew it would be impossible to use me for the on-camera commercial they might be shooting in the future, which would cause a conflict. Normally, print work has no union jurisdiction, but if a project involves shooting behind the scenes footage—or any video at all—and in instances like I just mentioned, unions can affect even print work.

How to Join: Let's face it if you want to pursue on-camera work whether it's commercials, film, or TV, you will need to be a union member. For some, they get lucky, and the opportunity comes quickly; for others, it can be a long and hard process. To join SAG-AFTRA, you must work on a union production at least three times while you are still non-union. This can be complicated as you're non-union, and they're only casting union actors on the production! This is where the Taft-Hartley Act comes in. Taft-Hartley essentially states that a producer can hire a non-union talent if they possess "a quality or skill essential to the role and an available union performer with the same quality or skill cannot be found." It sounds daunting, but can be done.

Once you have your three waivers, you are now officially SAG-AFTRA eligible. You now have a 30-day window in which you can do as much union work as you want (getting the higher pay rates without having to pay dues), but once that time passes, you become a "must join." Once you hit "must join" status, you are no longer able to work on union projects until becoming a member.

The Dues: At the time of this writing, to join SAG-AFTRA an initial payment of $3,000 is due immediately. There are also base fees of over $200 charged annually as well as work dues which are calculated at 1.575% of your earnings up to $500,000. For the current rates, check the SAG AFTRA website.

I focused on SAG-AFTRA here because it's so large and effects so many commercial actors and models. There are many other unions out there with different requirements to join and dues rates. Here are a few of the other major unions:

AGMA (American Guild of Musical Artists): This union represents opera singers, directors, ballet dancers, opera directors, and others associated with the opera and dance world.

AEA (Actors Equity Association): Many times referred to just as "equity," this union represents theater actors, rather than film and television.

AGVA (American Guild of Variety Artists): This union represents performing artists ranging from circus performers to stand-up comics, and cabaret performers.

FINANCIAL CORE: Fi-Core is a special status that allows union members to work both union and non-union jobs if an actor has a difficult time booking work. While this sounds ideal, there are many stipulations and complications that could cause you to lose the union status you worked so hard for – so fully research before pursuing *FiCore*.

No matter what union you are looking at, the issues are largely the same when determining whether or not it's a step you're willing to take.

—DAVID CARPENTIER—

Creative Art Director Interview

"If a model becomes the "Face" of a product or a service and is then seen in a conflicting market—The message will most likely be lost diluted or confused with someone else's message."
~ David Carpentier

Q: Do you always have a specific look in mind when booking talent? Has there ever been a time when someone totally opposite to what you thought you were looking for, booked the gig, and what are the criteria when choosing a model for a creative campaign?

A: I prioritize how people take direction and their personality over their looks when booking. Many factors, especially in the pharmaceutical market, affect why we choose a male or a female, whether they are in shape or not, their age, and ethnicity. These vary greatly depending on the US and global markets. But there are rules we must follow. Let's start with pharmaceutical products in the United States. When we decide on a "patient," it depends on the clinical trial's criteria on the approved FDA product. So, for example, product X is for heart disease. The clinical evidence and trials would capture the trends in who would be best suited to represent the disease. Males 45%, females 55%, Caucasian and Latino affected more by the disease from ages 35-50, limited exercise, and active in a career. So we haven't even got to the casting call yet concerning what is "the look." This already allows us to eliminate those who are too young, too old, too fit, and not the correct ethnicity, etc. It is important to note in the US, it is one market. Imagine how people may change or have to look so ethnically diverse that they have to represent many cultures from Europe, Asia, The Middle East, and Central to South America. My favorite description is Mediterranean. That basically means white with brown hair.

Believe it or not, often, we do not use children or pets in the advertisement because they are not included in the clinical trials for the product and would confuse the market if they are allowed to be on the product.

Not only do myself, the Creative Director, and my agency choose a model, we have the clients—usually many—and their medical and legal review teams input as well. They help us decide if the model we choose would be legally acceptable and represent the proper patient that would show up in the specific type of physician's office. By the way, this process may have started years before the photoshoot. We have figured ways of allowing some clients to think they are helping us choose to get who we want and others we have relationships where they just let us decide based on trust.

Q: What is the casting process?

A: Most of the time the models' agents do not follow the criteria, and I would say in every casting, 50-60% of the models/talent (Models are professionals, talent shows up and hopes to get work—a huge difference) do not even fit what the casting call requires. There are ways to quickly eliminate talent we would not choose, as creatives, we set interesting methods to preserve people's self-esteem while kindly having them leave a casting quickly. No matter what, we always have to cover a spectrum in casting, and we may see 200 candidates in a two day period and within 24 hours. Many times people don't dress right for castings. We'll ask arthritis sufferers to wear shorts or a skirt. I remember a funny time when we were doing an ad for arthritis, and a patient came in who had received a knee replacement. They didn't even have real knees, so how could they take a drug for arthritis? They had two giant scars on their knees. The agent didn't tell them this would be an issue.

Q: What role does stock photography play?

A: We start building the campaign from stock photography or CGI. The problem is sometimes we're so good at designing the stuff we do with stock photography that it goes onto market research and ultimately gets approved. The client wants the look of the model in the stock photo to be the person that represents the campaign. The reason they don't buy the stock photo outright all the time is because we want to have a library of shots, perhaps multiple angles, different wardrobes, outtakes. The advantage of having a shoot is that we can have a library of 100 shots. The disadvantage of having stock, even though it may be the perfect shot, is you only have one image. Stock imagery can sometimes be 50-55 thousand dollars for one image. This has forced photographers to come down a lot in their prices. There's been a weird battle going on for the last few years—stock photographers have become more expensive, and high-end photographers have started coming down in price. It's starting to change back a little recently, but for a while, computer-generated artwork became the thing to do. Looking back on it now, it was a really bad idea. The best stuff is photography and re-touching mixed with the tools we have now.

Q: Is it fair for an agency to ask a stock photographer to prepare what they're looking for, or is that cheating?

A: We wouldn't generally reach out to somebody who specializes in stock photography to use them. If we wanted to mimic their style and hire a photographer, we can get as close as we can, to a certain degree, but we have to refine it in a way that didn't look identical because it would still be considered copyright infringement. So if we try to mimic a shot of a woman on the beach with a wall that's lit for a certain time of day and waves that are hitting the shore in a certain type of way and we re-create something similar to the stock photographer, they can reach out and sue us for copyright infringement. We can engage the photographer from the stock site, say we like their stuff, and ask them to do the shoot for us.

Q: Can people copy shots and locations easily?

A: Technically, yes, but most of the time, people don't do anything about it. The only thing now that's become a real big issue is using landmarks with individuals. You have to get permission from the building to use the image. Sometimes the rates are incredibly high, sometimes you get lucky, and they're cheap. So we do our shoots now without using landmarks unless the client has a lot of money or the building is really old. You can use the Eiffel tower because it's been around forever, and everybody knows it. But if you did the Apple store on 5th avenue, you'd have to get the rights from Apple to have that in your advertisement because essentially you're using their name to promote you. You're using them to enhance the sale of your message. It used to be much more lenient than it is now.

We were going to use the Burj Al Arab in Dubai once for a shoot, and they asked, "what do you want to use it for?" We said it was a campaign for a pharmaceutical product and they asked what the product was. They researched it and said they believed in our product and it wouldn't be a problem. They said, "Can you send us what the ad will finally look like." We sent it. It was a woman on a sofa on the beach in front of the Burj Al Arab, they said absolutely not. I received a letter saying I offended Islam and me and my art buyer spent almost 3 months trying to clear our names to prove that we didn't intentionally try to offend Islam. The woman's legs and arms were showing, and they felt the couch was provocative. We found out the architect of the building was a Christian, and if you look at it in a certain light, it looks like there's a cross on it, so Saudi Arabia made them take it off their license plates. First they asked for $25k, then $250k, then they said absolutely not.

Q: Who has the rights to the Ad?

A: The client will always own the rights to the Ad, but the usage rights are negotiated with the photographer, model, artists, or any landmarks included in the campaign in 1-2 year agreements or full buyouts for either US/Global markets for web, print, TV, etc. When it comes to the model, if there is a full buyout, they will most likely not be allowed to work in competitive advertising for a specified amount of time. Often the models ask us for copies of the ad for their portfolio, and it varies from client to client, whether it can be used, or how.

In pharmaceutical advertising, it is even more complicated, essentially if the ad is being used in an uncontrolled public forum, it is considered a promotion and can have certain legal responsibilities/liabilities, so clients try to keep them only in professional communications that they, or their agency control. At the point where a model is used in a pharmaceutical campaign, they are a representative of the product and are used in sales promotions and sales materials that are far more vast than journal advertising. They become used in direct-to-physician sales, call materials, conventions, direct mail, digital details, and any other way you can imagine. We cut that down to 3-5. There are techniques through years of castings, where I have learned to hit that 24-hour time period to make selections, and it starts with the first model/talent at a casting call.

We work with production people and photography to kind of sneak people out. If we know someone isn't right immediately, we have command words that we say. We usually tell them to look straight forward, look to the left, come back, and give one big smile, which means we don't want them. The people give these big smiles without realizing they've already been counted out.

There have been instances where we did not expect to go in a certain direction. Sometimes it's purely based on personality, which is one of the first things I look for. I prioritize how people take directions and their personality over looks when booking. If you walk in the room and have a positive, smiling, confidence, and take direction well, I'd rather work with you then someone who looks good but doesn't know how to turn right or left and that happens a lot. You ask somebody to turn right, and they turn left, and one of the hardest things to do is ask somebody to smile on command. Most people can't do it.

There's a difference between "models" and "talent." Models know what they're doing. There's a circuit. We see the same groups of people all the time.

Q: How important is it that a model doesn't have a conflicting advertisement?

A: This is very interesting because I have seen many of the models I've worked with appear in non-competitive advertising shortly after I have worked with them. Depending on their contract negotiations, they are free to work in non-conflict advertising unless fully bought out, which essentially takes them off the market for 1-2 years. But it is critical that they do not show up in the competitive space or even look similar, especially in pharma. So much money and commitment are put into the promotions, and brand recall is critical when creating a brand. If a model becomes the face of a product or a service and is then seen in a conflicting market setting, the message will be lost diluted or confused for someone else's message and vice versa. In pharmaceutical, these patients represent the efficacy of a product in a certain disease state and the communications are highly targeted. We do a lot of competitive intel before we cast and go into market research to ensure that our message, models, and overall look and feel are distinct.

Q: Who makes the final call? Client or Ad agency?

A: This is very important. Ultimately the client thinks that they make the final call. Because they say yes or no, but it has to do with the relationship the agency has with a particular client. I develop a relationship with a client where they put their trust in me and let me make the ultimate decision. But there's a very specific system we have to go through for them to buy into it. In pharmaceutical, the medical and regulatory group, lawyers and doctors have to review every single advertisement. The person in the advertisement has to be reflective of how the drug actually works on people. As crazy as that may sound, if somebody has arthritis in their hands, they can't be holding something a certain way where it looks like their hand works perfectly. We bring this group in during the sketch stage and let them feel part of everything so they feel comfortable and that they've been part of the process the whole time. So ultimately, they make the decision, but we guide them the whole way. It's sneaky, funny, and a little bit cool, but we always end up getting what we want.

Q: How involved is the client in the creative process?

A: Recently, we've gone back to presenting the client with hand-drawn sketches, what we call 'tissues' because in advertising we used to be in the bar and draw ideas on napkins. Or they'd be on tracing paper and be very tough and very crude. We've learned that if we include the client in that process, we can guide them to buy into our story better because they've been involved since the beginning. But we're very specific in how we do it. We set-up certain ideas and present them in a certain order and a certain way so people won't automatically assume. Once they buy into a sketch, we go into the computer comp stage.

Q: What is the difference between digital or film?

A: The biggest thing now with digital is that we can get 3 to 4 thousand images from a 1-day shoot. It's a lot for us to go through, but we're marking images and watching things as we go. In the old days, it was more of a crapshoot because we'd take Polaroids as we were shooting film to make sure things looked right but we never knew what we were getting until the film was developed. It used to take 7-10 days to get images back from a photoshoot, now we're leaving with a hard drive with thousands of images on the same day. The next day we're already picking shots. So the digital age has helped a lot but also lost a little because since we get so many images, we spend less time setting a shot. So the art of it is missing a little bit, but it also gives us flexibility.

Q: How do you find American ads versus global ads with respect to freedom of creativity?

A: The ads in America are often based on cliché and wordplay so we're far more conservative in every way in advertising in America, especially with visuals. In a Viagra ad, a man was positioned behind a woman. That would never happen in America. Interestingly enough, in the Cialis commercials, when they show the two bathtubs side by side, the original concept was one bathtub with the man and the woman in the same tub. The regulatory group made them split it up because it was too provocative.

In the US, when we use language, we have to make sure it can translate into every single region. In Europe, it has to work in Asia, Africa, South America, and Latin America, so we can't use parlance or plays on words that are only familiar in America. They have to be factual statements. You wouldn't be able to say, "high 5" because that's only something that's understood in America. That doesn't translate to foreign countries. We also try not to use hand signals like peace signs, the way you fold your arms, and certain gestures because they can be seen as insults in other countries. We have to research all that. When we choose the talent in America, the talent is only based specifically on the drug itself and the specific demographic it works on most effectively. If 90% of the people who have the disease are Caucasian, our casting will be 90% Caucasian. If it also affects Asian people, we'll maybe put an Asian in it.

There are only two markets, the US and X US, which is the global market that includes: Europe, Asia, South America, Central America, Australia, and everything else. We try to find ethnicities representative of multiple regions so you can't tell where they are from. We call one look Mediterranean, which covers Greek, Italian, Middle East, and some places in South America. So when we shoot that one model, they can be used in 6 or 7 regions. When we shoot the Asian region, there are usually two different types of Asians we'll shoot depending on Malaysian style (Philippino) or China and Japan. There's always a Northern European look as well. We always have someone with blond hair and fair skin. That's a given. We may also try to have someone who looks Middle Eastern/Latino so they can work for both markets. For every campaign we do in America, if we have two models this means we'll need 12 globally. We don't create the same journal ad for other regions, we give them a template, and they use the artwork that's appropriate for the region, and they tailor the language to their region as well. In America, we control every aspect of the advertisement. In other areas, the agencies that represent the local areas get to change them, tailor them to the culture. Mediterranean covers Europe, much of America, and the Middle East. That's probably the biggest market because it covers so many areas.

Q: Do you get a market analysis and check for competing advertisements before you start a campaign?

A: The most important thing about a campaign is the competitive landscape, and I wouldn't necessarily call it competitive advertising. Before a campaign is developed, there's a good 12-18 months of strategic market landscape assessment that happens before we start the concept for what the campaign may be. We do an analysis of the market and existing ads by competitors. We study their advertising in the print market and TV too.

Confidentiality and timing are very important, therefore we sign legal agreements whether we talk about it or not. It's critical. We even sign nondisclosure agreements that if we work on a product, we can't work on a competitive product until 12 months after we leave the agency. We have to protect ourselves. It would be easy to go to a competitor and reveal strategies, so we're very careful to protect ourselves legally.

Q: Who chooses the photographer? Based on what criteria?

A: We pick photographers based on style. If they have a highly stylized, really contrasted imagery and that's what we want for our campaign, we'll lean towards that. If we want someone who can composite CGI along with photography and do studio composites, a lot of post-re-touching to make the campaign, we'd do that.

We have to triple bid every type of job out that's over 10,000 dollars so we're not just giving gifts to our friends. That said, there are ways of making sure the person you want to work with is the one you end up with. Again, this has to do with the trust and relationship you're building with your clients. You have to be fair, but you never want to put anything in the mix that you don't want or don't like. The budget also matters; the difference for the photographer could be anywhere from an average shoot, which is $150,000, to a high-end photographer whose going to shoot the same scene in the same amount of time that might charge $350,000. Relationships can also take 100k off a photoshoot if you really want to work with somebody.

—JULIAN MOLESSO—

Creative Director at H4B (Health for Brands) Interview

"Even with the new way we sell a brand, the medium may have changed. It's just not print and TV anymore. But it's still about the creative idea and you don't sell a brand you sell the experience of the brand."

~ Julian Molesso

Q: What is your company mission, and what is your position in it?

A: To do fearless work. To make the viewer say, "I want that brand!" My title is Creative Director.

Q: What is the process that comes to play when getting a new campaign?

A: There are many steps in developing a new campaign: First, the agency planners come up with a direction that is given to the creatives. Then the creatives come up with several concepts that are shown to the client. Once the client chooses several concepts, those concepts are put into market research, and along the way, those concepts may change a little. Then the winning concept becomes the new campaign.

Q: Who decides the market it's going to be geared towards?

A: The client and agency planners

Q: Do you usually have a specific look in mind when booking

talent? Has there ever been a time when someone, totally opposite of what you thought you were looking for, ended up as the face of the campaign?

A: Yes. Even before market research, the client and agency have a specific look in mind to represent their brand. And No, most of the time, that is the talent we usually book for the ad.

Q: Who has the rights to the ad, the photographer or the client?

A: The photographer has the rights to the photography from the ad.

Q: How important is it for a model to be cleared from another branding conflict?

A: That is very important. You don't want the same talent selling a brand just like yours.

Q: Who makes the final call, the client or the ad agency?

A: The Agency makes the final call.

Q: How do you find American ads versus European ads in respect to the freedom of creativity?

A: Creatively, the European ads are more creative and provocative.

Q: Who determines the rate and budget for the shoot and for the model/actor in particular?

A: The client has a budget that the agency will follow.

Q: How important is confidentiality and timing when creating a concept for a campaign, and do you ever find the influence of another company's current trend affecting your decisions?

A: It's all about being the first to own the market with innovative and fearless creative.

Q: Name a few projects that were extremely interesting in their creation process or outcome.

A: Since we are a healthcare ad agency, we have done campaigns for depression, HIV, and antibiotics that have changed the marketplace by becoming blockbuster drugs.

One thing to add; Even with the new way we sell a brand, the medium may have changed—it's just not print and T.V. anymore—but it's still about the creative idea, and you don't sell a brand, you sell the experience of the brand.

Mira Tzur

CHAPTER FOUR

—WHO CAN BE A COMMERCIAL PRINT MODEL—
& How to Get Started

The more you know yourself, the more success you'll have as a commercial model. By pitching to your strengths you'll be able to find the right representation and work for you. It's important to know your origin, type, age range, and special bag of tricks in order to stand out and thrive.

—FINDING YOUR NICHE—

—ETHNICITY—

Ad agencies usually gear a new campaign toward specific markets. Whether it's Hispanic, Asian, Caucasian, American, Middle-Eastern, African-American, or European, you want to know where you fit. This doesn't just mean your heritage but your look. For instance, I'm an Israeli sabra (born in Israel) with Polish-Russian heritage. Luckily I fall under the category of ethnically ambiguous. I work under five categories: Mediterranean, Hispanic, Middle-Eastern, Caucasian, and European—the more categories the more opportunities for work.

When you scan the QR you will see that the first two images represent a Hispanic, Middle-Eastern, or ethnically ambiguous appearance. The second two represent examples of European looks, and the last three are Caucasian looks.

—AGE RANGE—

Age ranges span 7-10 years, be sure to base your age on your appearance vs. your actual years. Unless an age is specified, for instance in liquor ads, cigarettes, or casino ads, you will rarely be asked for your true age. You always want to find out the range of a casting ahead of time, this allows you to either play up your youth or maturity to better fit the role.

Remember, commercial and or print lifestyle modeling progresses just as your own life does—it's a mirror of your reality. So if you are one to reach your forties or fifties—embrace it, don't try to compete with the jobs geared for the thirty year old. There are plenty of jobs out there for every age range. It is sure true that not everyone ages gracefully, therefore if you're one of the lucky ones who does, you'll find yourself working a lot more as you age, since the demand for such talent is bigger than the supply.

On September 24, 2016, California Governor Jerry Brown signed a landmark piece of legislation that directly impacts actors and entertainers. Law AB 1687, which was facilitated by SAG-AFTRA, states that the Internet Movie Database (IMDB) will be required to remove the ages of performers on their site should it be requested.

This legislation is a welcome development and one performers have long awaited. Age discrimination, whether intentional or not, is rampant in the entertainment business and this new law will make it increasingly difficult for casting directors to exclude a performer based on their age.

As I've mentioned before, casting directors aren't allowed to request a performer's age – and the consensus is to stick to an age range – as it should be based on appearance and demeanor rather than numeric age that should determine whether or not one fits a role. However, I've spoken with numerous casting directors who regularly view performers IMDB profiles and they admit to being influenced by a performer's age when considering their submission for a project.

SAG-AFTRA's Gabrielle Carteris, who shot to fame on the hit '90's show Beverly Hills 90210 as Andrea Zuckerman, was a driving force behind the new law. In a guest post for The Hollywood Reporter, Carteris wrote: "I would never have been called to audition for the part of 16-year-old Andrea Zuckerman if they had known I was 29. Electronic casting sites did not exist in 1990; today, they are prevalent and influential. Also, they affect casting decisions even when casting personnel don't recognize their unconscious bias."

Although numerous lawyers have questioned the constitutionality of the new law, and may try to get it reversed on appeal, it's a major liberating step, especially for the female sector trying to get younger roles and a groundbreaking achievement for all entertainers in general.

—TYPE CAST—

People will try to typecast you according to your age and ethnicity but you can broaden your range significantly by tailoring your appearance. Casting directors don't have time to use their imaginations when they're seeing hundreds of candidates in a casting session. Early on, I learned to make it easy for them to picture me in a role by understanding the character I was auditioning for and crafting my look for those specifications. It also helps to Google the client and see what types of looks they tend to choose. Some will want you to look your model best, others just want a real person. Tailor your look to those specifications and you will have a much better chance of booking the job.

—SPECIAL SKILLS—

Modeling isn't just about your face or measurements. Believe it or not, talent comes into play too. The larger your bag of tricks the better. Whether it's horseback riding or playing the violin, be sure your special talents make it onto your resume. It can be the difference between you and someone else landing the booking.

My dancing and fitness background has always helped me land work when the competition was tight but still, I became obsessed with adding special skills to my resume. On every trip, I'd insist on rock climbing, horseback riding, skiing, target shooting, and golfing just to add them to my bag of tricks. Back in the day, I even got my motorcycle license and when I got the chance, hit the range to brush up my shooting skills that I learned in the army just to check another box on the casting sheet!

There may be shoots where you find yourself in an uncomfortable situation, being asked to do something new and unknown. Use your judgment on this. For instance, I was in St. Maarten on a shoot and was dumped in the middle of the ocean to film a snorkeling shot. Not having snorkeled before, the fear had me borderline hyperventilating. My fake husband for the scene had to put up with my initial panic attack before I was able to tough it out—they got the footage and I got juicy lungs full of salt water!

The time spent in the Israeli army meant I knew how to handle a weapon. So when Rafael Defense Systems, an arms supplier to the military, was seeking a face for their brand, I was a natural fit since I knew my way around an Uzi and an M16.

Another time, it was my strength that was my asset for a national Macy's holiday spot. I was the only female able to swing a guy over my shoulder like Santa Claus. The client and ad agency confirmed my booking before I left the casting room, which is usually unheard of.

Harley Davidson was looking to do a clothing catalogue and it was my license to drive a motorcycle that booked me the job over another girl without a valid license. So you never know what special skill or asset will get you to book the job.

Below is a list of some common special skills but there are many more that your agency will be happy to know you can perform .

Skiing, horseback riding, dancing, singing, boxing, gymnastics, skating, martial arts, wrestling, yoga, bicycling, diving, golf, scuba, snorkeling, skateboarding, tennis, soccer, football, basketball, jogging, rock-climbing, musical instrument, foreign languages, driving, motorcycle-riding.

—GETTING STARTED AS A COMMERCIAL PRINT MODEL—

Now that you've determined your type, age range, and special skills, you're ready for the next phase. First, you'll need photos that represent you in various situations that fit your typecast. These pictures will be used on your composite card, online portfolio, and your agency's website. Next, you'll need to get an agent or agencies who will then send you on exclusive castings. A lot goes into this process so let's break it down:

—PUTTING YOUR BEST FACE FORWARD—

The photos you take will be a major factor for how agents and casting directors will perceive you and what kinds of clients you'll be considered for. So be sure to really consider your type and be realistic about what kinds of activities and brands you'd be representing with your age and look. You should get at least five to seven different looks at your first shoot so you have enough variety for your composite card or digital introduction email. Plan ahead; wardrobe and styling matter. It can be very beneficial to collect magazine articles and advertisements for inspiration. What brands and looks stand out? What can you see yourself realistically representing? This process will help you focus and narrow down the looks for the shoot so you get the most out of it. Once you've booked your session you've committed to this journey. Build momentum by fantasizing about the shoot, getting the clothes, researching what other models in your age range and category are shooting, and determine what's worth imitating and what's not. By the time you have your own shoot you'll have your own unique vision and original images. Plan to shoot with several photographers in order to get the strongest 16-20 images possible to get you started.

—HOW TO USE YOUR IMAGES—

Composite Card/E-Card

These are mainly for print/still modeling and advertising. A typical composite has one large image on the front and four smaller on the back. But nowadays, since everything is digital, it could be 3 picture design, maybe a 2-page collage, etc. The front image should be a headshot or three-quarter shot. For commercial composite cards, it is best to smile and have an approachable look. The opposite is true of fashion, where serious and aloof is the way to go. The four images on the back should show a variety of color and angles. These should portray you in different activities and motions to demonstrate your versatility.

Dogs, bicycles, babies, rollerblades, horses, balls, boyfriends, and any other props are a good way to show off your skills and emotions. At the bottom of the comp card, you would list the following measurements: height, bust/chest, waist, hips, shoes, and list your hair and eye color. These measurements are for the stylist to get your sizes correct if you book a job. Be accurate—you want the clothes to fit! Last but not least, list your agent's contact information. If you don't have an agent yet, put your contact and website information.

Headshots are used for on-camera commercial and acting work. This is a single image that should represent you accurately—the way you look when you go to the audition. You don't want a casting director to say you look nothing like your headshot so don't re-touch too dramatically, let your emotion and personality come through. Your acting resume will normally be taped on the back of the headshot, but again, most places will see this format digitally and won't ask for hard copy anymore.

—DIGITAL/POLAROID—YES, IT'S BACK—

With editing and re-touching technologies constantly evolving, clients are moving away from the trend of only requesting professional, re-touched images. While they want to see a polished book of images, they'll usually require untouched, unfiltered current digitals that represent exactly how you look without the help of Photoshop or the variety of editing apps that are out there before they confirm a booking.

—DIGITAL BOOK—

Create a portfolio with a minimum of twenty images that represent a rainbow showing your versatility. You can have these on an iPad or tablet to bring to castings. Models used to carry around a physical portfolio of their images, but those have long been replaced by smartphones and tablets. Google the latest apps for personal portfolio layouts and designs—luckily, there are plenty of options out there, including social media apps as your main online portfolio.

—ONLINE PORTFOLIO—

Several sites charge a small fee, monthly or annually depending on the service, that casting directors access to book talent. These sites include: Casting Networks, NYCastings.com, Actors Access, Backstage, Casting Frontier, Now Casting, Playbill, IMDBpro, and many more. This is a great way to be proactive for your career as these sites allow you to submit yourself to jobs. The images on these sites should show your diversity – different headshots depicting you in different age groups and characters. The more, the merrier!

—AGENCY WEBSITE—

Nowadays, all agencies have a company website with images of their talent, whether you're exclusive or freelancing. If you're freelancing, get with as many agencies as possible—it's essential to be on their company site. This is especially true with out-of-state agencies; they'll be relying on quality images on their website to direct-book you on jobs. The latest trend is that many out-of-town agencies ask you to upload social media pictures so clients can see how you really look when off the job and in your natural social environment.

This will sometimes require an initial fee of around $100-$150 depending on the agency—it's a small price to pay for having quality representation. You'll work with the agency to decide the proper images to use for their site.

—PERSONAL WEBSITE—

I'm a big believer in having a personal website. You can control how you represent yourself, the quality and number of your images, and your other talents you want to flaunt. Now many of us are multi-faceted; by having your site, you can list the different hats you wear. For example, my world of modeling is just one hat of the many I wear on any given week. By maintaining your website, you're able to uniquely represent yourself without having to fit in with an agent's or company's mold and image.

—SOCIAL MEDIA—

Facebook, Instagram, Twitter, YouTube, TikTok, and other social media sites have created an additional must-have platform for the modeling/talent industry. The world has watched and previewed unknown people rack up thousands and millions of followers and likes, simply by posting shots or videos of themselves posing, doing unique tricks, telling a story, flaunting a lifestyle, or simply feeding their pets—becoming internet sensations. With enough followers and organic engagement, companies will come calling.

We have all heard that a picture is worth a thousand words. *Instagram,* in particular, is a highly visual social media channel with one billion monthly active users. It's a massive platform all over the world. The perfect medium for brands to show their products and tell their story, all they need to do is to ensure that people actually see their Instagram images and that their brand ambassador is highly engaged and supported by their audience. Many well-known brands have built up sizeable Instagram followers themselves, from

Nike's 90mm, to Victoria Secret's 68mm, to Chanel's 36mm, to Zara's 34mm. All are savvy with their accounts; however, it is well beyond the capabilities for most average brands to reach higher traffic and audience alone, and they must work with hand-picked influencers. With that said, brands are constantly looking to find the perfect influencer match for their social media and branding vision.

*Scan QR code for categorized top influencer & brand ranking charts.

As you get to know me, you'll find I like to play the devil's advocate and always like to show the pros and cons of each medium. So don't get discouraged if you haven't started your social media channel, but do know that your presence in either one of these mediums is essential. It won't hurt you to choose one platform and start building your brand, as long as you are aware that some people will sometimes go to the extremes to gain social media followers at the expense of branding themselves as something they can't keep up with, or they may later regret.

Gaining real success in social media is tricky. Sometimes it's hard to measure and other times it's all over the media. But all in all, likes don't necessarily equal hefty paychecks and, more often, you might find yourself getting barter deals and free stuff more than monetary exchange for posts, especially at the beginning. It does get better with experience.

In the case that you are an advanced social media contributor, profiting from such can be a great way to add value to your personal brand or the one you represent.

I look at this business as a marathon vs. a sprint, as social media offers a lot of short cuts that industry veterans didn't get a chance to enjoy. Some highly successful influencers are making a lucrative career in various areas promoting food, travel, fashion, photography, lifestyle, design, sport, and fitness. Check out the ranking charts when scanning the QR above. This group of individuals are fortunate enough to have their voices heard in this highly competitive digital world, yet remain Anonymously Famous™.

Social Media Influencers Casting Example:

Product: Exercise Bike

Submission Date: TBD,
Location: Miami/NYC
Budget: Up to $20-$25,000 + Reasonable Travel
Services: Participate in 45 min spin class, 1 IG + 1 IG story set (2-3

slides), photos on site, pre-approved interviews
Talent Criteria:
Female ages 25-40 preferred
Social Footprint of a few hundred thousand or more
Likes to work out and is fun, but it's not her whole life

Breakdown: Looking for a fashionable media-worthy "it girl" or stylish "it guy" to participate in a social program (1 IG post that the brand will also pitch out) during that time. The talent should be 25+; however, if they are close to that age, and the brand is interested, we will work to make an exception!

Submission; Online/Self-Tape
Budget and Compensation: The brand has a budget that includes up to $10,000, in addition to two (2) guest passes, and three (3) nights at a hotel in Palm Springs.

—ACTING AND COMMERCIAL DEMO REEL—

While a headshot with a resume or composite card is great for print work, if you want to be taken seriously in the acting world, you'll need to create a demo reel. Such should be short and sweet, between a teaser and a trailer that lasts between 2-3 minutes. To prepare your demo reel, put your best material first. Make sure you aren't putting scenes that look like background work for another star. Remember, this is all about you. Make sure your choices are the best quality and in high definition. Label and credit each clip or scene. The key is always quality over quantity on a demo reel. If you decide to go with a demo reel that's a mixer of different clips, make sure to include a dramatic, comedic, and commercial clip separately to show your versatility. These days casting directors tend to prefer separate clips labeled with the show or commercial spot name so they can go directly to what they're looking for.

If you're just starting and don't have clips, try to shoot a scene with a partner. Many schools and casting places offer to tape you, so it looks professionally done. It's better to do this than use footage from extra or background work. Lastly, include your name and website or agent!

—FINDING AN AGENT—

An agent serves as a conduit between a client and a model. When a client releases a request for casting, the agent will immediately contact models or actors that fit the proper typecast for that role.

There are a few options to get in front of agents. Most modeling agencies will have an open-call once or twice a month and list the day and time on their websites. You can also register on the website, and they'll contact you if they can work with you. Most acting agencies participate in showcases where talent, for a small fee, can meet and greet agents and show their latest work with a monologue, scene, cold read, or commercial copy. These events are more common with on-camera agencies than print modeling agencies. All in all, getting any agent is easier with a good referral. A personal connection and recommendation is always the most effective way to get your foot in that coveted door.

—IS A MANAGER RIGHT FOR YOU—

If you're solely focused on modeling, then a manager probably isn't necessary. But if you're interested in any on-camera work, including film and television, you might consider having a manager juggle all the different agencies and appointments you're working with. In a nutshell, a manager will find you agencies and increase your level of industry exposure and audition opportunities. You are their product: they will package and market you, making sure your material is current and seeking the right roles for you. They have far fewer clients than your agents do and work more on all aspects of your career, taking a more personal interest in your development. Managers take on clients of varying types, so the good news is you're never competing for your manager's attention with someone just like yourself.

Another distinction is that managers can only establish a business relationship but not specify terms, whereas the agent has the authority to make deals with the client and negotiate contracts.

—TO BE, OR NOT TO BE EXCLUSIVE—

Freelance or signed

There are two options with agencies; you can be exclusive and work only with that particular group, or freelance and work with a variety of agencies. When you work exclusively with an agency, they are likely to be more committed to finding work for you. The relationship develops on a more personal level, and there is mutual interest in maximizing work and profit. There is no conflict of scheduling or competing agency or client interests. Most contracts require a base level of work opportunities, or you have the right to leave. On the other hand, when freelancing, you expand your client pool dramatically. Agencies only have so many clients, so by working with more than one, you are naturally exposing yourself to more opportunities. This is a good option for the more mature model—it takes a lot of juggling to manage multiple agencies, castings, and jobs, many of which conflict with one another. You act as your own manager, in a sense, rather than having a single person at a single agency directing your career—you're in the driver's seat. There's no right or wrong on this; each has its pros and cons.

—COMMISSION BREAKDOWN—

Now is probably a good time to mention that nobody works for free. The following are typical percentages that your agent or manager will require.

- Modeling agent: takes 20% fee from the client, and 20% from each booking.
- Acting agent takes 10-20% depending on your union status.
- Manager: takes 15% in addition to what your agent is already taking.

Keep in mind most modeling jobs will provide you with a 1099 at the end of the year, while others will provide a W-2 or W-4. You'll be responsible for reporting your taxes; your agent is not your employer.

—OUT OF AREA AGENCIES AND DIRECT BOOKINGS—

There are agencies all over the country that don't have a large pool of local talent to pull from. Once your book is well developed, you can work with these agencies, and they will book you directly from photos for out-of-town jobs. For instance, many New York-based models frequently work in Pennsylvania, Connecticut, Florida, North Carolina, Boston, etc. Every state has a unique focus; North Carolina does furniture shoots, San Francisco high-tech, Pennsylvania for appliances, Boston, Dallas, and Chicago are known for catalogs and department stores, and so on. While it's great that you don't have to attend a casting in person; you'll most likely have to send recent Polaroids or video before the client flies you in for the job.

—AVOIDING MODELING SCAMS—

Unfortunately, modeling scams are a major issue in commercial lifestyle modeling, even more so than in high fashion modeling. Child and teen models are more exposed to this than savvy adults, but it's still an issue at all levels of the industry. It's flattering when someone says your child is model material and that they are scouting for the next big campaign, but be aware that this flattery is often a scam. This has become such a prevalent issue that even governments are looking into these con artists. Federal Trade Commission for Consumer Information has conducted studies on the issue. According to the FTC, the following are major red flags:

1. You have to use a specific photographer. It's fine for agents to

recommend photographers they like but not okay that they take your money as the middle man and demand you use a specific person.

2.   A fee is required to start a relationship with the agency before they'll do any work on your behalf. The agency should only get paid a commission on the jobs you booked through them.

3.   You're told the opportunity could disappear if you don't act now. They'll make you feel guilty, saying that you're not serious about your career if you're not serious about committing now.

4.   They only accept cash or money order payments and guarantee a refund.

5.   They mention the big salaries you'll be making and guarantee work. Even successful, already established models have no guarantee in the frequency of their work.

— CASTINGS, AUDITIONS, AND GO-SEES—

Now that you've got your card, agent, and desire to get to work, it's time for your first casting. The number of castings will vary from week to week—you might have five castings in a day or only two in a week. This is normal. Let's decode some of the language to understand the requirements for each individual casting better.

—GO-SEE—

A go-see is only for modeling. You'll meet with the client or designer, show your book, and possibly try on garments or take some Polaroids/digitals. Be sure to bring your composite card and portfolio. You'll either be given a specific appointment time or a window of a few hours in which you may attend.

—PRINT CASTING—

Similar to a go-see, you'll take a few pictures with the casting director; nowadays, they rarely look at your book or comp card but bring them just in case. These castings are usually for advertising companies, and they care most about how you look in relation to the product they're trying to sell. You'll be given a time window in which to attend, depending on your category. I highly recommend coming at the beginning of your time slot. Sometimes, if the client sees what they want early, they may cut the session short.

—AUDITION—

You'll be asked to improvise a scene, read from a teleprompter, or perform a section from a script you've been given in advance or simply cold read. Your audition will be taped, and you'll leave your headshot and resume in some cases. You will usually be assigned a specific time for your audition because many times, the casting director will intentionally pair you with a pretend family, partner, or friend to test your on-screen chemistry.

During a callback for a recent Dropbox commercial, I was paired with two men, each assigned a different role. The person slated for the leading male role arrived late, allowing the other to show off his improvisational skills. They both booked the job, but the man originally slated for the lead was downgraded to a supporting role.

—DECODING THE DRESS CODE—

If no specific look is requested, always attend modeling castings in form-fitting clothing. For fashion castings, it's common to attend in all black clothing and heels. For commercial castings—print or on-camera—color is preferable as long as there are no distracting patterns and logos to detract from your look. It sounds crazy, but I Google the company for which I'm auditioning and try to dress in a color scheme consistent with the company's branding. I auditioned for Dropbox wearing blue, and Bank of America wearing red and booked both jobs. It just takes a few clicks to do your research and shows you are a professional that wants the job.

Normally shoots are conducted on a seamless wall, which means a white or grey background that projects or reflects more light. Occasionally, you'll have photos in front of a blue or green wall, these backdrops are used to import the desired background in post-production editing called chroma-keying, so consider something that will not clash. Trust me, I've made this mistake by wearing a blue top to a casting, and I looked like a bodiless floating head in the digitals!

Below are a few types you may be asked to represent at castings, so dress accordingly:

Cool hip professional, soccer mom, upscale casual, upscale business, upscale country club, not too modely vs. model type, girl next door, athletic.

An important thing to remember is there will be different looks required for different castings. There are days where you may have six castings. It's vital that you are organized, mapping out your day, and ensuring that you know where each casting is located and at what time. Have a bag with your different looks so you can tailor your style to each role you're trying to land. Take it easy on the make-up and jewelry and have clean, clear nail polish only—you should be a blank canvas that can easily morph into what the casting director is looking for. Tattoos, piercings, and tans limit your agent's ability to market you for the broad spectrum of jobs, so think twice before committing to these. On the other hand, a lot of companies these days look for unique characteristics such as tattoos and piercings or other distinguishing characteristics, but those can limit your job pool and are very specific requests.

—IFM MANAGER—

Ingrid French Management Interview

Q: How is your role as a manager different from an agent, and what's a manager vs. agent commission percentage?
A: My role as a manager is to counsel my clients regarding the industry and job opportunities, to present their materials to casting directors and decision-makers in the industry, to submit them for projects, and to work in conjunction with the other members of a client's team—their agent, publicist, lawyer, etc.— to make sure that everything is being done for my client that needs to be done. While an agent's primary job is to procure audition appointments or opportunities and negotiate contracts for a client, a manager's job is to do everything that needs to be done for a client to make sure their career is moving in the trajectory that client and manager have decided it should go, for it to be both financially rewarding and artistically fulfilling. Agents take a 10% commission. Managers generally take between 15% and 25% commission. I earn a 20% commission.
Q: How should a talent who seeks a manager get you to represent them?
A: I primarily meet clients through industry referrals from producers, directors, casting directors, and other clients who refer actors that they think would be a good fit for my office. I usually ask to see an actor's reel, their work, and all the materials they are using after looking at all the tools they are using, their profiles on online casting sites, personal website, and the IMDB profile, etc. I'll then determine if they are someone I'd be interested in meeting in person to consider working with. I also meet actors by going to

shows, theatre, industry events, and showcases, etc.

Q: What factors determine whether you'll represent a talent? Photos, personality, responsibility, looks, type, social media presence, or all of the above?

A: An actor or model's look or talent is usually the first thing that plays a role in determining whether I'll represent them. I go through their photos, resume, reel, social media, online materials, etc., and if I like everything I see, I'll want to meet them in person to get a sense of their personality and see if our visions for their career align.

Q: How much looks vs. talent play a role in signing a client, and how well do you need to know their work, strengths, and weaknesses?

A: Both an actor or model's looks and talent play a role in whether I'll sign them. I never want to bring someone on board who would compete with clients already on my roster, and I'm looking for someone with something unique about their look or talent that is exciting to me and something that I feel like the casting directors, directors, and producers will respond to and be excited about as well. There are usually one or more interviews with a prospective model or actor to determine their strengths and abilities and see if we'd be a good fit to work together.

Q: How important is it for talent to be exclusive to your agency vs. freelance when working with multiple agencies in your area, and, if exclusive, how long Is your contract, and do they have to be a union member?

A: Many of my clients are exclusive. For the clients that are exclusive to me, they can work with my office as management, and often they freelance through me with multiple agencies, increasing the prospective opportunities for auditions and jobs. Because my office is full service, we handle print, commercial, T.V., film, theatre, VO, and animation. If I'm only working with a model or actor in a specific area, then we may freelance because my contract encompasses all areas. Manager's contracts are generally two years long. I don't require someone to be a union member to sign them as my office works on both union and non-union projects.

Q: Do you find that a strong relationship with certain casting directors or agents gets you more castings for your talent, and should the talent be proactive to pursue such relationships once represented?

A: Relationships I have developed from my 20+ years in the business are among the most important things I can offer my clients. I have wonderful relationships with casting directors in the New York and Los Angeles markets as well as regional markets like the South East and international markets. These relationships mean that these casting directors trust me and depend on me to send them amazing talent that they'll send to their clients. I'll often have CD's reach out to me and say that they are only reaching out to a few reps, and they want to make sure my clients are considered. Likewise, the relationships that a model or actor has with a casting director are immensely important. To develop and cultivate those relationships is of utmost importance and something I work with my clients to make sure they are doing.

Q: Is it your job to keep track of image usage and contract expiration dates?

A: I do keep track of image usage and contract expiration dates, but I also always want to hear from a client if they come across an image or see an ad that they believe is past its usage expiration date. There are times when I'll have been told an ad or image isn't being used, and a model or friend of a model will see and alert me, and I can dig deeper and make sure that we are compensated for it any usage that we are owed.

Q: How have TV shows vs. films evolved the past few years with the increase of streaming services, and are there any special shows you love working on with your talent?

A: In the last few years, streaming services, cable networks, and other platforms for television and film viewing have exponentially increased the opportunities for actors, which has been incredibly exciting. Self-taping has also made it possible for actors to be considered for projects that they may not have otherwise been able to audition for. I love all of the wonderful opportunities for television that are in New York. It's incredibly rewarding to have clients book shows like Law and Order SVU that have been staples in NY for many years. It's also wonderful to have clients on shows like Billions, Succession, and Hunters. It's exciting to see a web series get picked up for television and see client passion projects find homes on streaming platforms.

—JESSE ROSALES—

Reality TV Casting Director Interview

Q: What are the first steps a casting director needs to do when getting a new project?

A: It depends on what kind of project; print/ commercial, film/T.V., reality T.V., etc. Though I have experience as a talent manager that casts print, commercial, and small film projects, etc., I've been focusing on casting and development for reality T.V. in the past ten years, so I'll speak on that medium.

Depending on if a project is already green-lit or still in development—it all comes down to finding the right characters. For The Food Network's, Chopped, which I had the pleasure of casting for 17 seasons, we reached out to practically every outlet we could find that was relevant in the

Mira Tzur

food/hospitality world. During casting for our first season, I personally cold-called every single restaurant involved in NYC's Restaurant Week to see if their chefs were interested in applying for the show. I also built relationships with culinary schools, PR firms specializing in hospitality, and chefs and restaurant owners alike to help spread the word about casting.

In general, when you first get a new project, you must make sure you're on the same page with the client's vision and what it is that they are looking for. A lot of times in reality television, you're looking for a typecast. Maybe a contributor for a dating series, a chef to compete on a cooking competition show, a fitness trainer who can coach people on losing weight, etc. Once you know what you're looking for, you get the word out about your casting any way you can. Social media, talent websites, etc.; however, a lot of the time, a great find comes from personal contacts.

Q: What kind of projects have you worked on as a casting director?

A: I first started out casting print/commercials in 2006 as a casting assistant. I cast a Sprint and Verizon commercial and then started working at a modeling agency, first as an intern, then I was promoted to agent's assistant. I left there and started interning for a casting director who specialized in finding hosts and experts for various clients—a big one being QVC. He was hired by FUSE Network to cast their new video DJs and hired me as his assistant. We then cast a dating show for them. After that project was wrapped, my next project was serving as a casting assistant for The Food Network's hit cooking competition series, Chopped, on which I worked my way up to casting director and spent 17 amazing seasons finding awesome chefs to compete on the show. I've had the pleasure of casting hit shows like *MTV's* True Life, *Bravo's* Real Housewives of New York City, *TLC's* BBQ Pitmasters, and *NBC's* Biggest Loser.

Q: What are some of your highlights from casting sessions, and what are the basic steps in this process, from getting the phone call from the client or ad-agency to making the phone calls to the agencies and scheduling the casting day(s)?

A: For reality T.V., I send out casting calls, and there are various networking groups that casting directors can post their projects on. From there, people apply, and if we're interested in hearing more, we set up a time to chat. Most casting interviews these days are over video—especially if the person is not local, or in a studio setting. For Chopped, we had dedicated offices to bring local chefs in to put them on-camera. If we were looking for chefs in New Orleans, we would fly there and interview chefs locally. From there, what we would say is, "No news is no news" meaning it can be a long process. We have to cut down those interviews into 2-3 short casting videos, write a pitch about why this person would be good for the show, send out said pitches to the client, and wait to hear their feedback.

Q: How often do clients attend castings, or do they mostly rely on

the photos and video you send?

A: It's mainly digital, and the client rarely interacts with the talent before the booking. However, the client, Bravo in this case, would want to meet with the new potential housewife with *Housewives of New York* before committing to offering her a role on the show.

Q: In a typical casting, how many applicants do you see for each breakdown, and how many agencies do you reach out to?

A: It all depends. With Chopped, we were tasked with casting three seasons at a time, so we would constantly be interviewing chefs for 2-3 months while reaching out to find specifics for special episodes like teen chefs for a teen episode, lunch ladies, charity workers, etc.

Q: How have websites like casting networks and actors access changed the casting process, and is it easier or harder for your casting process?

A: I utilized Casting Networks and Actors Access while casting for MTV's long-running hit series, *True Life*, which did garner some interesting candidates. With the internet, it makes things a lot easier because my casting web reaches the entire country as opposed to just my neighborhood block.

Q: When a client hires you, do they usually have specific ideas about who to cast, or do they rely on your expertise and just provide sketch or storyboard for the campaign, and how much influence do you have over the client's decision?

A: As a casting director and development producer, it's my job to identify talent and interesting concepts that could potentially be turned into a series.

I was working as a development producer for a production company who had an excellent relationship with *MTV International*. We were in a one-on-one session discussing host options for a series she already had in mind, and during our conversation, I suggested an entirely different series—with talent attached—revolving around a food and music concept. I showed her tape on the talent and said, "This is the show." That was on a Monday. Tuesday, I brought in the talent to the production company, and we were at MTV headquarters on Wednesday. The show sold and is now going into its third season.

I deal with talent directly, and I find that is the best way to go about the casting process. I build relationships with my talent, and they trust me to take care of them. I'm not an evil T.V. producer who is out to get people and make them look bad. I treat my talent like family. They are my babies, and I only want what's best for them. If they want to do a show, I will hold their hands and walk them through the process as best I can. What I expect them to bring to the interview are their sparkling personality and good energy.

Q: Does it make a difference whether the model/actor is working as a freelance or with an agency, and does your relationship with the agent influence who you invite to a casting?

A: I treat all talent the same—with the utmost respect.

Q: Share a few of the projects you cast that left a lasting impact.

A: I have to say I truly loved casting, Chopped. It's a fun, feel-good show where the drama is in the cooking. It helped so many people share their stories, and I feel like we've had a big part in making some culinary celebrities.

The show is in its 31st season, so I'm very happy and proud of the work I contributed to making that show a long-running success.

—ELAINE DELVALLE—

Casting Director Interview

"I expect talent to show up prepared, knowing the part and ready to take direction."
~Elaine DelValle

Q: What does a casting director do?

A: A Casting Director is responsible for finding talent to place in projects that include commercials, feature film, television, theater, print, voiceover, and reality.

Q: What kind of projects have you cast?

A: I have cast for all of the above.

Q: What are some of your highlights from casting sessions, and what are the basic steps in this process from getting the phone call from the ad agency to calling agencies to scheduling the casting day(s)?

A: My favorite aspects of casting are discovering talent, encouraging growth, and working with each actor to help them achieve the role. I am fulfilled when my client is wowed by the talent I bring to them.

The basic steps in my process are: From the moment I get the call with a client's needs, I deep-delve to understand the job thoroughly so that when I put out a breakdown to the agencies, managers, and actors, all is clear from the moment we say go. I need to know the pay scale, the usage, the union jurisdiction, etc. Moreover, I take a deep dive into the scripts and whatever else my client makes available so I can deliver what they want and pepper my delivery with great surprises.

I use casting platforms like *Breakdown Services, Actors Access,* and *Casting Networks* to post my breakdowns. I review submissions, photos, reels, training, experience, resumes, etc. and schedule auditions with those actors most suitable for the roles at hand. I either schedule actors for an in-studio read or request the actor self-tape for the role.

The latter is my favorite. I like to give actors the opportunity to send me the video that they think best represents them in the role. It allows actors to see their own work and send me exactly what they intended from a performance. Great performances always stand out. I reserve in-room auditions for callbacks or chemistry reads in which I pair actors up. I send my client a digital link to see all of the best auditions. Their top choices become a callback or direct hire. In callbacks, the client is usually in the room or live via internet stream. I schedule and run the session doing everything I can to facilitate the best audition from every actor and the best experience for my client.

The final step is booking the talent. I expect talent to show up prepared, knowing the part, and ready to take direction.

Q: How often do clients attend castings, or do they rely on the photos and video you send now that it's all digital?

A: In this day and age, I seldom have clients in the room with me on the first round of casting. I can move much faster without them there.

They tend to want to get to know each person, and rightly so, but those moments are not on tape, and so that hinders efficiency when getting actors in and out. The callback and chemistry reads are when the client is usually in the room.

I allot much more time per audition for callbacks and chemistry reads, but each client is different, so I work in any way that is best for the client. I have long been an advocate of virtual casting. I recommend that every actor get familiar with self-taping, so they can finally have a say in what the casting director and client sees. I believe it is a gift when actors are asked to self-tape. You'd be surprised how many actors don't actually take that opportunity. Also, those self-tapes come with deadlines. Not delivering your self-tape in time for the deadline is the equivalent of being late for an audition. It makes me work harder to have to accommodate their inefficiency.

Q: In a typical casting, how many talent do you see for each breakdown, and from how many agencies do you request to see talent from?

A: I allow submissions from all agencies. There have been some people that I have experienced as being hard to deal with, and so I limit intake from those. I would not want my client to suffer the consequences of an uncooperative participant. Productions are intricate; talent or their reps should not introduce a problem. They should be the solution. I can receive thousands of submissions for each role, so I have to be efficient and effective with my time.

Some roles are harder to fill than others, so for those, I go as far as posting my casting search on my Instagram. One such role was so hard to fill that I even went on a local television station to promote the search. I was especially proud to have discovered the talent that met that role's needs. It gave an opportunity to an inner-city kid that may have never known the world of professional entertainment.

How many talent I see always depends on how much time I have to fill the role. I leave no stone unturned.

Q: How have websites like Casting Networks and Actors Access changed the casting process? Is it easier or harder for you?

A: *Casting Networks* and *Actors Access* have made it easier but also harder. Easier because of the reach that I have and the speed at which my breakdowns go out—the video platforms are professional, and I am proud to share them with my clients. But, there is always a downside; the downfall of technology is that it takes jobs away from people. I used to need assistants, readers, studio space, but in today's world, I can work an entire casting from my in-home office at my computer.

Q: When a client hires you, do they usually have specific ideas about who to cast, or do they rely on your expertise and simply provide sketch or storyboards for campaigns and films, and how much influence do you have over the client's decision?

A: I respect their boards and ideas very much. I want to make my client feel that they have been offered what they are looking for. That said, I still consider myself an artist, and give myself the leeway to add those additional actors that are a total departure from the initial idea but still a great option for the role. The clients are pleasantly surprised by a changeup that can either reinforce their original ideas or give them a new perspective. I have often found that clients don't know what they want until they see it.

Q: What is the protocol for calling a talent directly? What do you expect talent to bring to castings?

A: I seldom call talent directly unless they are self-represented. I reach out to agents in the way that they deserve and expect. I expect talent to arrive on time and prepared. I don't want to hear about excuses. I just want to get to the work and move on. Regardless of how great an actor did, I still have to get to my next appointment and keep the day running on-time.

Q: Does it make a difference whether the model or actor is working as a freelancer or with an agency, and does your relationship with the agent influence who you invite to a casting?

A: It does in that when an agency has signed you on, it means that the actor or model has passed their test. The actor represents them as much as they represent the actor. I expect to see greatness when an actor that is signed to a legit SAG-franchised agency walks through the door. I have come to expect them to be the most prepared and best trained. They tend to be the whole package ready and eager to work. The same goes for the big modeling agencies; even their second-tier models are usually better than anyone that is freelancing.

I also attend lots of acting school showcases so I can discover talent. I like to know that actors have put the work into their craft and are not just depending on their looks. Acting is technique. Acting for camera requires both raw and technical talent. An actor that has honed their craft is truly one that I will be happy to see repeatedly until I find the right role for them.

Q: Share a few projects you cast that left a long-lasting impact.

I have cast many projects. I believe that any role that has provided an actor with great reel material has a lasting impact.

I once discovered an actor at a film festival, where his Spanish language film played. I knew it was just a matter of time before I'd have him in a role. I ended up giving him his first English language role. The reel material from that project lead to a much bigger role as a series regular.

Another instance is when I booked a couple of young adult actors in a proof of concept pilot. Their work in those roles lead to bigger things, and one is working as a series lead while the other is in a major blockbuster due out next year.

I've been known to tell actors, "I told you so," in the best of ways. It is easy to spot that special something when your career is about seeing talent. Most recently, I did an all-out search for a Latinx adolescent girl. I found her through my social media, and by the time this book comes out, she will have learned that she will be the lead in a new SAG-AFTRA series. The stories go on and on. It is truly a pleasure to work with so many talented people.

Like most casting directors, I began my career as an actor so I can relate to the love and dedication to craft. I have also written, directed, and produced film, so I come to every job with a unique understanding of those aspects of the work.

Actors should realize that casting comes after and during many other aspects of the filmmaking process. They are just a small portion of the puzzle that has a huge impact on the whole.

—ROMONA PITERA—

Model & Talent Agency Interview

"In the world of commercial print, knowing your typecast and how you can manipulate your looks can be helpful. Having acting skills increases your chance of booking the job because your personality and confidence are helpful for making your "look" shine through the room."
~Romona Pitera

Q: How should a model who's seeking representation get connected with your agency?

A: We accept submissions online through our website. We also accept submissions by referrals from our clients and models. Perceptive models need to submit a resume, professional commercial headshot, and two other contrasting photos if you have them. Digital images are accepted, but they should show you smiling.

Q: Which factors determine whether you'll represent a talent? Photos, personality, responsibility, looks, or all of the above?

A: Usually, a great smiling commercial headshot and a strong acting resume, along with their special skills, will do. We look for inspiring people to work with, someone that I'm excited to send to my clients, and that is excited to be going out on our casting calls. Your attitude and professionalism determine if an agent can trust you to go out on their casting calls and if they are eager and willing to do what they can to make it to a casting or last minute booking.

Q: Do you think models that are also actors have a better chance to book commercial/print jobs?

A: Yes, usually, they have a much more successful career because they can improvise in a scene, and that can lead to becoming the face for the product in the commercial ad as well as the print ad. Also, photographers and directors remember stand out talent and will often request to work with them repeatedly.

Q: When a casting comes in, how do you prioritize your talent phone calls?

A: I reach out to the talent that are reliable and are always willing to do what they can do to attend the castings. They juggle their time as much as they can.

Q: How many models do you represent?

A: Currently, on our website, it shows we have 1,200 models. However, that does not accurately display how much talent is available to us. I would say we have approximately 1,000 active models and actors.

Q: What is the male/female ratio?

A: Approximately 45% men and 55% women.

Q: Which age range do you find gets the most castings?

A: It's hard for me to give an accurate answer because we represent talent from teens to seniors. We are known to have a variety of talent in all age ranges and ethnicities, and I think that contributes to our company's success.

Q: How important is it for talent to be exclusive to your agency versus freelance or working with multiple agencies in your area?

A: We do not require our talent to be exclusive to us. I believe it is our business relationship, that is important. I will hustle for my talent and expect the same in return from them. I think, over time, you realize who is the right agency or talent for you.

Q: Do you find that a strong relationship with certain casting directors gets you more castings?

A: Yes, absolutely. It's important to have a strong working relationship with casting directors. Just as I look for my talent to be reliable, that is also what the casting directors are looking for from their relationship with agents and talent. Helping them meet their casting needs for their clients is very important. Essentially we are all working together; clients, casting directors, agents, and actors.

Q: What's the timeframe in which talent can expect to get paid?

A: Typically, it takes 45 to 90 days to receive payment for print jobs. However, it depends upon how the client decides to pay, are they sending the payment themselves to the agency directly or are sending the payment through a paymaster.

Q: Is it your job or the talent's job to keep track of image use and contract expiration date?

A: Yes, the talent is required, especially if they freelance, to keep track of the product they are advertising and the usage, where the image will be used in advertising, and how long the client has the right to use the image.

Q: What's an agent percentage vs. a manager percentage?

A: For modeling jobs, the modeling/talent agency takes 20% from the talent's rate, and a manager takes 15% from the talent.

—LAUREN GREEN—

Talent Agent Interview

Q: How should a model who's seeking representation get connected with your agency?

A: Send digital pictures to our office. Headshot, full length, and a specific shot if the talent specializes in an area.

Q: Which factors determine whether you'll represent a talent. Photos, personality, responsibility, looks, or all of the above?

A: All of the above if we are in need of their look at the time.

Q: Do you think models that are also actors have a better chance to book commercial/print jobs and how much do looks versus talent play a role in signing a client?

A: It depends on the talent. An actor has experience with expressions and relating to the camera. My agency does not sign talent, and with each project that we work on, it's both the look at the time and the talent of the model to express themselves as directed.

Q: When a casting comes in, how do you prioritize your talent phone calls?

A: We work on all calls the same way, in a timely manner.

Q: How many models do you represent? What is the male to female ratio?

A: Approximately 700. Half & half.

Q: Which age range do you find gets the most castings?

A: We represent all ages & it varies from week to week. There is no real answer to that.

Q: How important is it for talent to be exclusive to your agency versus freelance?

A: We freelance with all our talent.

Q: Do you find that a strong relationship with certain casting directors gets you more castings?

A: Everyone has their favorites, and you would hope that all the agencies get the same projects, but that is not always the case.

Q: What's the time frame in which talent can expect to get paid? Is it your job or the talent's job to keep track of image use and contract expiration date?

A: Talent payment for commercial print is 2-3 Months. Here at my agency, we contact everyone as soon as the payments are in, and I do my best to have my talent paid as fast as possible. It is up to the talent to follow up on getting a copy of their work. We follow up on all expirations of each project the best we can.

Q: What's an agent percentage vs. a manager percentage?

A: An agent receives 20% of the gross of the booking.

—BOOKING CODES—

Congratulations, your agent called, and you're on hold for a job! What does that mean? You are asked to hold the specific dates you committed to at the time of the casting. You are not allowed to book other work on those specific dates. Normally, you will receive a confirmation or a release within a few days. Sometimes, you will have a second client that wants to hold you for the same dates. That means you have to tell the second agent you are on a first right of refusal for his client—within a few days, you will know which job you booked. Once you've confirmed the job you're not allowed to set time limits and required to be available. Your word is your bond, don't back out of your commitment. Don't make any plans or other bookings the day of the shoot. No one can predict how long a shoot will run as so many factors are involved in each step of the process. This is especially true for on-camera commercials that can often run into the night.

—PROFESSIONALISM & INTEGRITY—

So much goes into planning every shoot from its conception that you need to understand the audition doesn't stop at the casting call or the booking. Even though you landed the job, there's a high expectation for you to be as professional as the rest of your competition. You want to be easy to work with, positive, engaged in the project, and with the people on set. After all, much of this industry, or any other, is about relationships. If word gets around that you're professional to work with, more jobs will naturally come your way.

Be sure to get a lot of rest before a shoot, the night before a big job is not the time to party. We've all got twenty-four hours in a day, and you should use them wisely. It's ok to say no to your friends and remain disciplined—this is your career. Also, remember when you leave the set, the advertising agency and client will continue to remember your work and behavior long after the shoot, so leave on good terms and make every impression last.

—OTHER TIPS TO REMEMBER—

1. Don't change your look between your audition and shoot day.
2. Be on time, even early to set.
3. If you are asked to bring wardrobe, be sure you have what is requested, ready to go in advance.
4. Be sure that all releases and contracts are agreed upon before the shoot.
5. Don't gossip about people on set or involved in the project—no negativity!
6. Don't be on the phone unless during specified breaks.
7. Often there's a lot of "hurry up and wait." This doesn't mean you can disappear; you are expected to be ready to work at all times.
8. Your professionalism represents your agency's reputation.
9. Don't negotiate rates and terms with the client. That's what your agent is for.
10. Some projects would love you to flaunt it on social media, others will ask you to sign an NDA (Nondisclosure agreement), and you won't be able to discuss the project until it's out in the open. Most of the big jobs will want to keep the surprise, especially for competition and copyright reasons. So just check in advance before spoiling it or getting in trouble with production.

"The impression you leave in your wake will be a lasting one."
~ Mira Tzur

Below are a few examples of casting notices you may receive from your agency. Notice the details and breakdown of roles and usage :

EXAMPLE 1:

CLIENT: Crest
TIME: 9 am-4 pm

LOCATION: Photographer studio

PRODUCT: Crest Professional
USAGE: 3 YR GLOBAL USE
RATE: $3000
SHOOT DATE: TBD

ROLE: Hygienist

Age: 40-50— Gender: Female

Ethnicity:

- Should look like someone who is either from the US or Europe.
- Brunette or dark hair.
- Caucasian, but skin should not be too much on the light side.

Looks:

- Should look like the woman next door in her 40's.
- She should be well maintained.
- Definitely not super thin and not glamorous.

Face:

- Should give out positive vibes, should have a genuine and nice, truthful smile (e.g., smile with her eyes too, not only her mouth)
- She should have nice, clean teeth.
- She should give you a warm feeling when you look at her.

EXAMPLE 2:

CLIENT: Major Finance/Investment Brand

LOCATION:
One on One Studios
34 West 27th St. – 11th Floor
Between 6th & Broadway

RATE: Session: Adult: $1500 session day
- Session: Child: $1000 session day
- Usage: Adult- $1500
- Usage: Child-$1000
- Travel: Adult: $500/day
- Travel: Child: $500/day

USAGE: 2 years US unlimited digital media and print media to include but not limited to OOH, internal and agency promotion. No video, no broadcast

TRAVEL / OVERNIGHT: Monday, Sept 7th **
SHOOT DATES: Sept 8th and 9th **
SHOOT LOCATION: Lancaster PA

NOTES: PLEASE READ
- Talent will be asked to option Travel & Shoot Dates Sept 7th -10th. Talent would potentially travel evening of Monday the 7th; however, shoot dates may push. Please Make sure talent is available and on option, and please let our assistant know of your status at sign in.
- Talent may shoot 1 or 2 days TBD.
- Please only one parent or guardian to accompany the child to audition.
- We will be scanning for any Finance brand conflicts at the sign-in.

DRESS:
Talent should come camera-ready with a comp card or headshot for the client. Photographer and creative both prefer modern, eclectic style. Think an eclectic J Crew style, not too upscale, but simple, clean lines, great pattern, interesting, flattering cuts, but still very much relaxed like for a day out in the country. Hair should be down. Kids should be clean, presentable, but not upscale and too stiff.

EXAMPLE 3:

CASTING DATE:

CLIENT: Infiniti (the car)

LOCATION:
Three of Us Studios
39 West 19th st.
12th floor, between 5th and 6th Ave.

PHOTOGRAPHER:
AD AGENCY:

SHOOT DATE: August 8, 2014

RATE: $3500

USAGE: Usage: one-year www, unlimited rights, (excluding broadcast)

USAGE OPTIONS EACH ADDITIONAL YEAR - $2,500
2 additional years up front - $5,000
HOUR DAY: up to 10 hours on location in the New York area.

General: The hero in this ad is the CAR; the people are in the background dining with the celebrity chef. They are picking seven talent. All actors should be believable as chefs, restaurateurs, urban aesthetes, aficionados. They should be stylish, international types: self-assured, successful entrepreneurs. No heavy people. They are not fat, but normal or slender
These are people who have lived.
They go back to the beginning of a 15+ year career. Casual luxury.

1. Every person must know his category. They must come adequately prepared in terms of knowing when and what category they belong in.
2. DRESS GENERAL: UPSCALE CASUAL. For women, no bear arms, no skirts above the knee, no skin below the clavicle bone. Men in button-down shirts and nice pants, no ripped jeans. If they must wear jeans, they should be very nice, dark jeans. Jacket for men might be nice too. Nice shoes. Women in blouses and long skirts or slacks. No sneakers or flip flops. Dress should be as if you are going out to dinner or a gallery opening. You have taste and

style. You don't shop at old navy.
3. Talent does not need to bring a headshot or comp card. We will not be taking them. Please tell them this. At this point, it slows down the process.
4. 4. Please spread your people out in the given time period! DO NOT GIVE THEM THE ENTIRE TIME PERIOD. IE 3:20, NOT 3-3:45.
5. For EVERYONE: hair down and natural. No ponytails, pigtails, clips, updos, etc.

CATEGORY A: Caucasian Male, age 35-45
CATEGORY B: "Global Citizen"/mixed-race, ambiguous race Female, age 40-50
CATEGORY C: Middle Eastern or Mediterranean Male age, 40-50
CATEGORY D: African American Male, age 40-50
CATEGORY E: Caucasian Female, age 35-42
CATEGORY F: Chinese Male, age 40-50 …not Japanese

This is just one example of what you'll be asked to fill out—prior to a print casting or non-union commercial:

General Information

Name_____
Address_____
Phone_____
Email_____
Date of Birth_____
Age Range_____

Specs:
Size_____Hair_____
Eyes_____Weight_____
Height_____Waist_____
Bust_____Hips_____
Shoes_____

Union Status: Circle One
SAG, AFTRA, AEA, SAG Core, SAG Eligible

Ethnic Appearance: Circle all that apply
Caucasian, African American, Middle Eastern, Hispanic, Asian, Ethnically Ambiguous

SKILLS
Sports
Examples: boxing, skiing, swimming, weightlifting, scuba, aerobics, dancing, golfing, etc.

Music/Dance_____

Language/Dialect/Accents_____

This is the form you fill out upon arriving at a commercial audition for a union role.

And here is an Exhibit E, Audition Sign-In Sheet for Union Commercials

SAG·AFTRA ONE UNION

EXHIBIT E
COMMERCIAL AUDITION REPORT

PAGE _____ OF _____

TO BE COMPLETED BY CASTING DIRECTOR

(X) WHERE APPLICABLE ON-CAMERA ☐	PRINCIPAL PERFORMER ☐ OFF-CAMERA ☐	EXTRA PERFORMER ☐	AUDITION DATE
INTENDED USE		Person to whom correspondence concerning this form shall be sent: (Name & Phone Number)	
CASTING REPRESENTATIVE NAME	COMMERCIAL TITLE - NAME & Ad-ID®		ADVERTISER NAME
PRODUCT	JOB NUMBER	ADVERTISING AGENCY AND CITY	PRODUCTION COMPANY

INSTRUCTIONS: For 3rd and 4th Auditions, please note for which role the performer is reading. If 3 or less performers are called back for that role, and none is on a 1st audition, no payment for the 1st two hours would be due. Completion of the required information is necessary for performers to receive the following audition-related payments: 1) overtime, 2) 3rd and subsequent auditions for principals, and/or 3) audition/interview payments for extras.

PERFORMERS ARE REQUIRED TO SIGN IN AND SIGN OUT, WITHOUT EXCEPTION.

* SPANISH LANGUAGE TRANSLATION SERVICES

TO BE COMPLETED BY PERFORMERS

NAME (PRINT)	*	MEMBERSHIP NUMBER OR SOCIAL SECURITY NUMBER	AGENT (PRINT)	ACTUAL CALL	TIME IN	TIME OUT	INITIAL	CIRCLE INTERVIEW NUMBER	ROLE (IF 3RD OR 4TH AUD.)	SEX (X)		AGE (X)		ETHNICITY (X)					PDW
										M	F	40+	-40	AP	B	C	LH	NA	(X)
								1st 2nd 3rd 4th											
								1st 2nd 3rd 4th											
								1st 2nd 3rd 4th											
								1st 2nd 3rd 4th											
								1st 2nd 3rd 4th											
								1st 2nd 3rd 4th											
								1st 2nd 3rd 4th											
								1st 2nd 3rd 4th											
								1st 2nd 3rd 4th											
								1st 2nd 3rd 4th											

This recorded audition material will not be used as a client demo, an audience reaction commercial, for copy testing, or as a scratch track without payment of the minimum compensation provided for in the Commercials Contract and shall be used solely to determine the suitability of the performer for a specific commercial.

AUTHORIZED REPRESENTATIVE SIGNATURE:

The only reason for requesting information on ethnicity, sex, age, and disability is for the talent union to monitor applicant flow. The furnishing of such information is on a VOLUNTARY basis. The Authorized Representative's signature on this form shall not constitute a verification of the information supplied by performers.

Asian/Pacific	– AP	Latino/Hispanic – LH
Black	– B	Native American – NA
Caucasian	– C	Performer with Disability
Other	O	-PWD

Mail one copy to SAG-AFTRA on the 1st and 16th of each month.

WHITE COPY-UNION

Audition Sign-In Sheet Exhibit E Commercials 5.8

MODEL RELEASE

1 of 2

DATE:	SHOOT LOCATION:
MODEL NAME:	SHOOT DATE/CALL TIME:
MODEL AGENT:	CLIENT:
AGENT CONTACT:	PRODUCT:
AGENT ADDRESS:	JOB #:
AGENT PHONE:	FEE:

In full and complete consideration of the fee specified above I, the above-named model (the "Model"), hereby grant to (the "Agency") on behalf of the above-named client ("Client"), and their respective licensees, agents, successors and assigns(Agency and Client collectively referred to herein as the "Licensed

Parties"), the right to use my services (the "Services") throughout the world as provided at the above-referenced shoot (the "Session") per the following terms and conditions:

1. The Licensed Parties shall have the absolute right to copyright or publish, or use model's name or likeness or recorded voice or picture, portrait and any other likeness of model, whether in whole or in part, or composite or altered character of form, or illusionary effect, in conjunction with my own or fictitious name, in the territory (the "Territory"), media (the "Media"), and for the term (the "Term" described herein to advertise and promote the product, which is considered a sensitive use.

2. Media: The photographs or film taken of model at the session may be used in any professional or consumer media, including but not limited to print publications, direct marketing materials, point of purchase, digital media and materials and internet, and any other media specified in the Special Provisions/Options provision herein.

3. Special Provisions/Options: Unlimited all Global trade media to include but limited to print ad, agency client promotion, collateral, patient materialism DM, FSI, postcards, trade show, health fair, POS, POP, web/internet (global by nature), tablet, apps, any and all electronic/digital and new media, social media, displays. To be used by all and any agencies

4. Model agrees that during the Term, Model will not allow model's likeness to be used in advertising competitive with the product (s) featured in the advertising created in connection with the Services provided hereunder.

5. Model agrees that the above-referenced payment covers payment for my services and for travel, meals, and incidental expenses, if any, during the entire period of production as well as the rights specified herein.

6. Model waives any right, title, or interest in or to the photography likenesses produced by the Licensed Parties. Model further agrees that no materials produced in connection with this Model Release need to be submitted to model for approval.

7. Model warrants and represents that this license does not in any way conflict with any existing commitment on model's part, and understand that nothing herein will constitute any obligation by the Licensed Parties to make any use of the rights set forth herein. Model's right to perform

Services under this Model Release, or to grant the rights granted hereunder, and model agreed to hold the Licensed Parties and their respective affiliated companies, officers, directors, shareholders, and employees harmless against any claims arising to of breach of model's warranties hereunder.

8. Model acknowledges that model is an independent contractor, and that model shall be responsible for the payment of Federal and State income or other applicable taxes. Model further warrants that model is 21 years of age or older.

9. This Model Release must be signed on its face by Model, or Client has no obligation to submit the payment specified herein, No variation of any of the terms of this Model Release, or payment due hereunder, will be effective unless in writing.

10. Model agrees to hold in strict confidence all details of this assignment, or any information that may be disclosed to model either orally or in writing by the Licensed Parties in connection or incidental to the Services Model may provide hereunder. A breach of this provision shall be considered a material breach of this Model Release.

11. Model understands that model may not use the photographs from the assignment or Shoot for portfolio or other purposes of self-promotion without express written permission from agency with approval from client.

12. I have read and understand the terms of this Model Release, and that this Model Release constitutes the entire agreement between the Licensed Parties and me regarding the subject matter and that under no circumstances shall I, my beneficiaries, administrators, executors, or assigns have any right to maintain any cause of action or demand against the Licensed Parties arising from the terms of this Model Release.

ACCEPTED AND AGREED:

_____Signature_____ Date_____
Printed name of model

IF ABOVE MODEL IS UNDER 21, PARENT OR GUARDIAN MUST SIGN BELOW

I am the guardian of the above-mentioned minor. I consent to the foregoing on behalf of such minor and personally join in the warranties and representation set forth above. I also agree to indemnify and hold harmless with respect to any

Mira Tzur

claims, which the minor may make as a result of the exercise by the licensed parties of their rights here under.

I verify that the above model is 12 months of age or older.

ACCEPTED AND AGREED

_____Signature_____Date_____
Printed name of Parent or Guardian
Witnessed by_____Signature _____ Date_____
Printed name of Witness

Below are a few samples of model/talent voucher/invoice, sometimes needed in addition to the agent contract, as proof of actual work .

VOUCHER

NUMBER 77920

TALENT AGENCY

MODEL: _____

DATE: _____.___

INVOICE TO:

Name: _____

Address: _____

City: _____ State: _____ Zip: _____

Attn: _____

Photography to be used for any of the following uses must be checked below, or the release is not valid.

☐ Brochure   ☐ Billboards   ☐ Point of Purchase
☐ Catalogue   ☐ National Ad   ☐ Product Packaging
☐ Other (specify) _____   ☐ Internet

Bonus to be paid: _____

Length of time Ad will run: _____

RELEASE

In consideration of RECEIPT OF PAYMENT, IN FULL, of the model-talent fees stated herein, I herby give my permission for the above named clients to produce, copyright, and/or publish my photograph or image as specified under Job Description for a period ending _____. If payment in full is not made within thirty (30) days, client DOES NOT have the rights to use my photograph or image. Use of my image or likeness for billboards, counter cards, posters, displays, packaging, television, non-broadcast videos (industrial), national consumer advertising, interactive media, or use on the internet must be included in Job Description and will require a separate usage fee. Photos are not permitted to be used for stock. In the event of a dispute, the prevailing party will be entitled to attorney fees.

We are agents for the models and talent we represent and as such, ARE NOT their employer of record. We are not responsible for any withholding taxes, workman's compensation or unemployment insurance.

THIS RELEASE TAKES PRECEDENCE OVER ANY RELEASE SIGNED AT THE TIME OF JOB WITH THE EXCEPTION OF CONTRACTS AND AGENCY RELEASES THAT CONTAIN THE SAME INFORMATION HEREIN.

BILLING INFORMATION

TYPE	DATE	TIME		RATE	FEE
		FROM	TO		
FIT		—			
JOB		—			
JOB		—			
JOB		—			
BONUS		—			
TRAVEL		—			
O.T.		—			
LINGERIE		—			
OTHER		—			
SUBTOTAL			▶		
AGENCY FEE 20%					
REIMBURSEMENTS:					
TOTAL DUE			▶ $		

CLIENT CONFIRMATION
All work as described herein has been fully completed and all billing information is correct and uncontested.

Release is not valid until payment is made in full.

_____   _____
MODEL • TALENT SIGNATURE   CLIENT SIGNATURE
OFFICE COPY – WHITE • CLIENT COPY – YELLOW • MODEL'S COPY – PINK

102

INVOICE TO:

Name: _____

Address: _____

City: _____ State: _____ Zip: _____

Attn: _____

Photography to be used for any of the following uses must
be checked below, or the license is not valid.

_Brochure   _Billboards   _Point of Purchase
_Catalogue   _National Ad   _Product Packaging
_Other(specify) _____ _   _Internet

Bonus to be paid: _____

Length of time Ad will run: _____

LICENSED USE

In consideration of RECEIPT OF PAYMENT, IN FULL, of the model-talent fees stated herein, I herby give my permission for the above named client to produce, copyright, and/or publish my photograph or image as specified under Job Description for a period ending _____. If payment in full is not made within thirty (30) days, client DOES NOT have the rights to use my photograph or image. Use of my name, image, or likeness in any manner not specifically enumerated in the Job Description, including but not limited to billboards, counter cards, posters, displays, packaging, television, non-broadcast videos (industrial), national consumer advertising, interactive media, or use on the Internet will require a separate agreement and a separate usage fee. Photos are not permitted to be used for stock. In the event of a dispute the matter will be submitted to binding arbitration pursuant to the rules of JAMS, before a single neutral arbitrator, experienced in print talent agreements, applying, the laws of the State of New York and the prevailing party will be entitled to reasonable attorneys' fees and costs.

We are agents for the models and talent we represent and as such, ARE NOT their employer of record. We are not responsible for any withholding taxes, workman's compensation or unemployment insurance.

THIS LICENSED USE WILL SUPERSCEDE ANY OTHER CONFLICTING DOCUMENTS BETWEEN CLIENT AND TALENT.

BILLING INFORMATION

TYPE	DATE	TIME	RATE	FEE
JOB		FROM TO		
BONUS		FROM TO		
TRAVEL		FROM TO		
O.T.				
SUBTOTAL		→		
Don Buchwald & Associates, Inc. AGENCY SERVICE FEE 20%				
REIMBURSEMENTS:				
TOTAL DUE	→ $			

CLIENT CONFIRMATION

All work as described herein has been fully completed and all billing information is correct and uncontested.

PERMISSION FOR USE IS NOT GRANTED UNTIL PAYMENT IS MADE IN FULL

Model/Talent Signature _____   Client Signature _____

Model/Talent Print _____   Date _____

EMPLOYER

103

SAG-AFTRA Theatrical Wage Table

		2.5%	2.5%	2.5%
	07/01/16-6/30/17	07/01/17-06/30/18	07/01/18-06/30/19	07/01/19-06/30/20

Day Performers

Performer	$933	$956	$980	$1,005
Stunt Performer	$933	$956	$980	$1,005
Stunt Coordinator (employed at less than "flat deal" minimum)	$933	$956	$980	$1,005
Airplane Pilot (Studio)	$1,248	$1,279	$1,311	$1,344
Airplane Pilot (Location)	$1,622	$1,663	$1,705	$1,748

Weekly Performers

Performer	$3,239	$3,320	$3,403	$3,488
Stunt Performer	$3,479	$3,566	$3,655	$3,746
Stunt Coordinator (employed at less than "flat deal" minimum)	$3,479	$3,566	$3,655	$3,746
Airplane Pilot (studio and location)	$3,479	$3,566	$3,655	$3,746
Airplane Pilot (flying/taxiing - daily adjustment)	$1,070	$1,097	$1,124	$1,152

Multiple Picture Performers

Performer	$3,239	$3,320	$3,403	$3,488

Background Actors

Schedule X, Part I	$162	$166	$170	$174
Schedule X, Part II	$162	$166	$170	$174

Special Ability Background Actors

Schedule X, Part I	$172	$176	$180	$184
Schedule X, Part II	$172	$176	$180	$184

Stand-Ins / Photo Doubles

Schedule X, Part I	$189	$194	$199	$204
Schedule X, Part II	$189	$194	$199	$204

Swimmers and Skaters

Schedule X, Part I	$373	$382	$392	$402
Schedule X, Part II	$418	$428	$439	$450

Updated as of 11/28/2018

SAG AFTRA Theatrical Wage Table

Singers (Employed by the Day)

Solo and Duo	$1,010	$1,035	$1,061	$1,088
Groups 3-8	$886	$908	$931	$954
Groups 9+	$774	$793	$813	$833
Mouthing 1-16	$741	$760	$779	$798
Mouthing 17+	$576	$590	$605	$620
Contractor 3-8	50%	50%	50%	50%
Contractor 9+	100%	100%	100%	100%

Singers (Employed by the Week)

Solo and Duo	$3,239	$3,320	$3,403	$3,488
Groups 3-8	$2,971	$3,045	$3,121	$3,199
Groups 9+	$2,703	$2,771	$2,840	$2,911
Step Out				
(Per day - up to 15 Cumulative bars)	$504	$517	$530	$543
(Per day-16+ Cumulative bars or detained 1 hour+)	$1,010	$1,035	$1,061	$1,088
Contractor 3-8	50%	50%	50%	50%
Contractor 9+	100%	100%	100%	100%
Choral Group Call-Out for 5 Bars or more	$56	$57	$58	$59

Term Performers

10 to 19 Weeks Guaranteed (per week)	$2,780	$2,850	$2,921	$2,994
20 Weeks or More Guaranteed (per week)	$2,314	$2,372	$2,431	$2,492
Beginners: 0-6 months	$1,248	$1,279	$1,311	$1,344
Beginners: 7-12 months	$1,393	$1,428	$1,464	$1,501

Stunt Performers (Employed Under Term Contracts)

10 to 19 Weeks Guaranteed (per week)	$2,780	$2,850	$2,921	$2,994
20 Weeks or More Guaranteed (per week)	$2,314	$2,372	$2,431	$2,492

SAG AFTRA Theatrical Wage Table

Dancers

Daily Rates

Solo/Duo	$933	$956	$980	$1,005
3-8	$818	$838	$859	$880
9+	$714	$732	$750	$769
Rehearsal	$550	$564	$578	$592

Weekly Rates

Solo/Duo	$3,001	$3,076	$3,153	$3,232
3-8	$2,752	$2,821	$2,892	$2,964
9+	$2,502	$2,565	$2,629	$2,695

Stunt Coordinators – Theatrical (Employed On A "Flat Deal" Basis)

Per Week	$5,722	$5,865	$6,012	$6,162
Per Day	$1,451	$1,487	$1,524	$1,562

Mira Tzur

CHAPTER FIVE

—NUTRITION & WELL-BEING—

W hen it comes to health and well-being, everything starts from the inside out. Younger people might be able to fake it, but as you age, nights of drinking alcohol and eating pizza will begin to show on your face and hips.

Looking back, since I was physically active as a dancer, I allowed myself to eat more than I would if I were less active. These eating habits caused my weight to fluctuate frequently, which became frustrating for someone in my profession. Around that time, I was also a personal trainer and had clients that sought more information about diet and nutrition. All these reasons inspired me to delve deeper into the study of health and nutrition and become a Certified Natural Health Professional (CNHP).

Becoming certified at the Institute for Integrative Nutrition, required me to complete my studies of iridology, body-works, nutrition, herbal supplements, and naturopathy, among other things. In the following chapters, I'll share the major pillars of my nutrition and fitness knowledge to inspire you to live a clean life that thrives both personally and professionally.

The following are my personal essentials for keeping great health. I'm not revealing any secret or miracle here, but sometimes we neglect to adhere to these basic rules.

1. Sleep: 7-8 hours minimum
2. Drink lots of water: coffee, juice, and wine don't count. You need 8 glasses of pure water. For every cup of coffee or glass of juice you drink, you should follow it up with a glass of water for proper hydration.
3. Eating a balanced diet
4. Exercise: I'll elaborate on exercise in the next chapter
5. Mental and Spiritual health: keeping mind and body at equilibrium. We'll delve deeper into this in chapter seven.

—NUTRITION—

Ever wonder why a well thought balanced diet is so hard to keep?
With our constantly on-the-go lifestyles reaching to whatever is frequently available in a rush is no surprise and rarely results in healthy choices. I try to prepare my food in advance and plan ahead to avoid bad dietary decisions. I do my best not to shop when hungry because I end up stocking the pantry with junk food instead of nutrient-rich fruits and veggies. Most importantly,

I try to think of diet as a lifestyle and not a fad program. I'm conscious of balancing all the elements of my diet: carbs, protein, fats, vitamins, and minerals.

—DIETS—

Not all diets are created equal. Whether or not we are aware of it, dietary choices are based on various factors, including: origin, background, religious beliefs, clinical needs and restrictions, weight management, nostalgia, advertisements, or simply built-in habits.

Here's a list of some diets you may have heard of:

- Raw food aka raw foodism
- Calorie counting
- Eat by blood type
- Detox diet: Gluten-free/Casein-free/Ketogenic
- Low fat/low carb/low calorie
- Vegetarian
- Portion control
- Food combination diet
- Belief diet based on: philosophy/religion/ spirituality (kosher, halal, Buddhist)
- Atkins/Zone/Weight-Watchers/Nutri-System/Jenny Craig/Fit for Life
- Pyramid (king, prince, pauper)
- Ketogenic diet
- Mediterranean Diet
- Paleo Diet

I've personally tried many of the diets listed above and have found what works for my body. I like to incorporate certain aspects of multiple diets into a balanced one, not a radical approach to healthy eating, one that served me well over the years. The food combination diet, which strategically combines food groups for maximum nutrient absorption, is a favorite of mine. For my metabolism, the pyramid diet—also known as King, Prince, Pauper method—is also best, meaning my heaviest meal is in the morning, lunch a medium portion, and dinner is on the lighter side.

—MAKING PROPER CHOICES—

We don't always have the answers about how the food we eat ultimately effects our health, but I know for sure I make my food choices that stack the odds in my favor. My Rules are simple: choose whole, unprocessed, organic, pure, fresh foods. I ask myself, "what do I know for sure?" Well, I know that the body is like a sports car that requires the highest quality fuel otherwise it will not perform optimally. Thus, I set my standards high and constantly looking for trusted and likeminded farmers, entrepreneurs, brands, and products that will deliver on the promise to provide a fuel with uncompromising standards. I refuse to settle for mediocrity.

Most doctors will agree that 90% of chronic health issues are due to inflammation on a cellular level. What foods have anti-inflammatory properties? Greens, grasses, tonic herbs, adaptogens, antioxidant-rich super fruits, seaweeds, and medicinal mushrooms among others. I love it all and I have it all as my daily health regimen. For example, Ultimate Elixir was designed for a modern busy person who has no time to be squeezing celery juice on the way to the airport. But the convenience of putting a scoop of a product into a bottle of water and drinking that on the way to the airport takes away all excuses.

—MY FAVORITE MEALS FOR MAXIMUM NUTRITION—

—BREAKFAST—

1. Cooked oats: (bran, steel-cut groat, rolled or instant) are all great, especially before a workout. Oats have a low glycemic index that is important when exercising as it promotes slow digestion while burning more fat. Oats are known to prevent diabetes, with low cholesterol and high fiber, the cholecystokinin hormone that's released helps feel full longer.

2. Fruit shake: Fruits are a great way to start your day because they digest in twenty minutes and don't take much energy. I love adding either a spoon of tahini (polyunsaturated fat) or avocado (monounsaturated fat, both different kinds of healthy fats or ground flaxseed and psyllium husks, my great additions to promote regularity. As for the base, almond, cashew, oats, or coconut milk are ideal vegan base choices for me.

3. Banana: This complex carb is great if you're on the run or short on time. Bananas have a high content of vitamin B6, magnesium, and potassium. Such an important mineral that helps lower blood pressure and gives a great energy boost. I like adding a few almonds to lower the absorption of sugar.

4. Eggs: High in protein, and vitamin D. Studies have shown that the

healthiest, most filling way to eat an egg is boiled. They are also great in veggie omelet combinations or, my personal favorite, an egg omelet with 2 spoons of *Quaker Oats* or quinoa, making it the greatest pancake treat.

—LUNCH OR DINNER—

Rule of thumb: make sure to include vegetables in every meal. The high fiber and mineral content helps break food down and keep you feeling full and satisfied. In general, you can't go wrong by combining vegetables and protein. Here are a few of my favorite meals.

1. Quinoa, kale, watermelon, and edamame salad: gluten-free and packed with protein and fiber.
2. Low carb/low-calorie wrap: Turkey avocado or turkey hummus. These are great food combinations. While the avocado is high in unsaturated fat and Vitamin E, turkey is low in fat and carb content while being high in protein. Hummus is also high in protein and fiber and easy to make; it's a great way to punch up the flavor in your wrap.
3. Big salad with protein: I try to have a salad for dinner every day. I use all the fruits and veggies in my fridge. Focus on different colors of greens as well as cucumber, tomatoes, pickles, artichokes, peas, and fruits. Almonds, sunflower seeds, or a little goat cheese or feta can add a kick to your vegetables but don't overdo it on the higher calories foods. For protein, add chicken, salmon, or tuna. Vegetarians can substitute tofu, quinoa, tempeh, or seitan. I like to sauté mushrooms with brussels sprouts and carrots to add on top. Don't negate the health benefits of your salad by dousing it in high-calorie grocery store dressings. A simple salad dressing I like combines ginger, balsamic, oil, water, mustard, and agave.
4. Shakes: I like making spirutein shakes since they have high vitamin and protein content but are low in carbs and calories. This low glycemic index food can serve as a meal or a snack.
5. Sushi: Try to go for sashimi but when ordering rolls, stick with brown rice over white. The bran layer, which gives rice its brown color, has all the vitamins, minerals, and oils. White rice lacks all the fiber and health benefits of brown rice.
6. Homemade veggie soup: Veggie soup is a great way to cleanse your system and give your body a break, especially in the winter. Don't wait to get sick before making a homemade soup. Be creative! You can make a big pot and have a healthy go-to meal ready in moments. By adding different spices to your soup, you add not only great flavor

but also boost your immune system. I'll discuss the power of spices a little later. Scan the QR to see some of the meals.

MIRA'S HEALTHY MUFFINS

Ingredients:
1 cup super-seeds: Chia, Golden flax, Red Quinoa, Hemp
3 large bananas
1 shredded apple
3 shredded carrots
1 tsp baking soda
1 tsp baking powder
1 egg
1 tsp vanilla extract
1 cup *Quaker Oats*
2 cups brown rice flour/almond flour
1 cup milk (coconut, soy, or almond)
Optional: *Stevia* for added sweetness

In a large mixing bowl, combine all ingredients. Fill muffin cups ¾ and bake at 350 degrees for 20-25 minutes.

—MIRA'S SUPERFOODS—

"Certain food will fill you but not fulfill you. Make sure to choose wisely."

1. Almonds: Almonds have been shown to actually lower the glycemic index of other foods when consumed together. They're also packed with antioxidants and, believe it or not, protein. They contain six fatty acids that boast a wide range of health benefits. Soak them in water overnight make them grow larger and also easier to digest— this is true of all tree nuts since they are seeds after all. If you eat an ounce of almonds before a high-starch meal, they will help to reduce your blood glucose level and cholesterol. Studies have shown almonds help with brain development, weight loss, and provide a good energy boost. I've never seen so much diversity in a single food

source.

2. Avocado: This fruit has the fiber and monounsaturated fat that you need to fuel post-workout. They're high in potassium and protein, low in carbs, and have no sodium or cholesterol. Avocados are delicious with veggies and fruits, raw or grilled. They are very versatile and mix well with a variety of sweet or savory foods. I even add them to shakes and make avocado muffins.

3. Quinoa: This superfood is gluten-free. It has more vitamins, fiber, iron, and antioxidants than any other grain. High in vitamins B & E as well as calcium, quinoa is considered a complete protein and has all 9 essential amino acids. It comes in different colors, but unlike rice, all colors of quinoa are nutritious.

4. Dark steamed greens: Kale, spinach, and broccoli are all cancer-fighting powerhouses that help detoxify your body. They are high in iron and folic acid, which are especially important nutrients for women. Vitamins A, C, and K are also found in these foods. I like to steam my veggies, but you can also eat them raw.

5. Blueberries: One of the highest antioxidant foods on the planet; these little berries are known to prevent cancer and help fight heart disease. Blueberries also contain Vitamin C, fiber, and manganese, which are essential for all beings and aids in bone development and strength. I add them to everything I can: shakes, salads, or my famous muffins.

6. Sweet potato: Not to be confused with yams, these are among the most nutritious root vegetables. They're high in vitamins A, B, and C, as well as calcium and potassium. The high level of carotenoids is what gives these veggies their orange color. These are delicious grilled or pureed with cinnamon, Japanese Furikake, or Thai chile lime spice.

—SPICES ARE YOUR BEST FRIEND—

The use of spices and herbs as natural healing remedies have been well documented throughout history. The following are my go-to spices:

1. Garlic: This is a natural antibiotic, and studies have shown it can help lower blood pressure and prevent heart disease. This is my instant remedy the minute I feel cold symptoms coming on. This herb's immune-boosting power has been well known for centuries, and as my grandmother made sure to teach me, it's a vital addition to our diets.

2. Ginger: Naturally anti-inflammatory, great for our skin and digestive system. Used deliciously in tea, salad dressing, soup, and various

foods and sauces I lovemaking.

3.   Cinnamon: Has both anti-bacterial and anti-inflammatory properties. High in fiber and antioxidants, cinnamon helps lower cholesterol and prevents blood clots. An excellent addition to both sweet and savory foods – sprinkle some on mango or sweet potato it's delicious.

4.   Cayenne: You're probably familiar with cayenne pepper as one of the ingredients of the master cleanse. This pepper shrinks blood vessels and boosts metabolism. Anti-inflammatory and filled with antioxidants, Cayenne also helps to neutralize the acidity in your diet.

5.   Turmeric: A member of the ginger family, turmeric is the spice that gives curry its yellow color. Considered a superfood that helps improve the circulatory system and benefits both skin and bones, it is also no surprise it is getting lots of attention as a natural cancer fighter.

6.   Sage: Believed to enhance memory, sage is anti-inflammatory and packed with antioxidants. It helps boost insulin and reduces blood sugar, which is beneficial in preventing diabetes. I like to drink a sage and rosemary tea; it's my delicious way to enjoy the benefits of this herb.

—MIRA'S TIPS TO CONSIDER—

No doubt, eating 3-5 servings of fruits and vegetables will improve your health and the way you feel. A variety of colors and choices is the smart way to go. Each color has different benefits – here's a list of the veggie rainbow.

a.   Red, blue, and purple: these are responsible for memory function, vitamin A, C, and potassium. They have the anthocyanins pigments that are found in cranberries, kidney beans, beets, strawberries, red peppers, cherries, eggplant, and tomato.

b.   Orange and yellow: These colors are high in beta-carotene and vitamin A, which are great for your vision. They're also high in vitamin C, which, as we all know, is a big immune booster. Papaya, oranges, lemon, corn, yams, and pineapple are good options in this category.

c.   Green: Leafy greens contain vitamin A and K as well as calcium. These fruits and veggies are well known for their disease-fighting benefits. Green beans, zucchini, kiwi, grapes, apples, kale, and spinach.

d.   White/tan: These are a good source of riboflavin and niacin, which are known for boosting energy production and also contain high levels of antioxidants. Mushrooms, onion, cauliflower, banana, ginger, and garlic are all good choices.

I believe in 5 small meals a day to keep your metabolism running—especially if you work out. Apples, bananas, low carb, and a low-calorie protein bar, avocado, or a handful of almonds are all good options.

—DECODING NUTRITION LABELS—

To make their products seem healthier, many companies use deceptive tactics on the nutrition label. Understanding how to read these labels is vital to make the right food choices. In this section, I'm going to explain how to read and understand each category of the food label.

Nutrition Facts			
Serving Size Servings Per Container			
Amount Per Serving			
Calories	Calories from Fat		
% Daily Value			
Total Fat	g		
Saturated Fat	g	%	
Cholesterol	mg	%	
Sodium	mg	%	
Total Carbohydrate	g	%	
Dietary Fiber	g	%	
Sugars	g		
Protein	g		
Vitamin A	%	Vitamin C	%
Calcium	%	Iron	%
Percent Daily Values are based on 2,000 Calorie diet. Your daily values may be higher or lower depending on your Calorie needs:			
	Calories	2,000	2,500
Total Fat	Less than	65g	80g
Sat Fat	Less than	20g	25g
Cholesterol	Less than	300 mg	300 mg

Sodium	less than	2,400mg	2,400mg
Total Carbohydrate		300g	375g
Fiber		25g	30g
Calories per gram:			
Fat 9	Carbohydrate 4	Protein 4	

The first mistake people make when deciphering food labels is only looking at the fat and calories listed. These don't tell the real story.

Serving size is the first thing to take note of. It's not regulated and up to the manufacturer to decide what serving size to use. Serving size is usually a familiar measurement, for example, one slice of bread or 1 square of chocolate. Make sure to be aware of how many serving sizes are in what you plan to consume – many times what appears to be a single serving, say 1 muffin, is 2 serving sizes, so you need to double the calories listed to determine the true calorie count of the muffin.

- Calories are units of energy. The number listed on the label is the number of calories per serving.
- Fat: To obtain the true percentage of fat, you multiply calories and fat and multiply that number times 100.
- Cholesterol, sodium, carbohydrates: Stay on the lower side for these nutrients. Watch the percentage number.
- Fiber: Having a high percentage of fiber in your diet helps keep your digestive system regular. 5% or less is considered low.
- Sugar: Notice there's no percentage for sugar. Because sugar impacts your health negatively, there is no recommended amount to ingest because it's unhealthy.
- Protein: There is no daily value suggested for protein because everyone has different physical needs based on their body composition.
- Vitamins: Be sure to get enough vitamins in your diet. 20% or more is high; the more you can increase your vitamin intake towards 100%, the better. Notice vitamins A, C, calcium, and iron are an essential part of food labels. Others are optional.
- Percent Daily Values: This section is a guide to help you establish whether a serving of food is high or low in a particular nutrient. These reference numbers are based on a 2,000 calorie diet, but even if you consume more or less than that, %DV is still a valuable resource.

Calories Per Gram. This lists calories per gram in fat, carbs, and protein. For example, say you have a 200 calorie nutrition bar with 12 grams of fat, and 9 fat calories per gram. By multiplying 12x9, you reach 108, which tells you that 108 calories of the bar are total fat calories. The same equation applies to carbs and protein.

—INGREDIENT LIST—

More important than the nutrition label is the ingredient list. For example, when you buy rice, the ingredients listed should only be rice and no other additives.

—FALSE ADVERTISING—

"Fat-Free": This usually means fat has been substituted by something else. Most of the time, the substitute is an unnatural additive with no nutritional value. For example, in fat-free salad dressing, they add sugar to make up for the lack of fat. Fat is a good thing, as long as it's coming from healthy sources like oils and avocado. The best quality oils are in a dark container because they are sensitive to light, heat, and oxygen.

"Low Sodium": Canned goods are notorious for high sodium counts due to salt and MSG (monosodium glutamate), which are added to flavor and preserve. Salt and MSG are extremely detrimental to our overall health. Soups and other canned food many times claim to be low or lower in sodium but are still high in sodium, just not as excessive as the original product. Companies will also decrease serving size to mask sodium counts.

"Sugar-Free": Sugar in cookies, cakes, and other foods is replaced by artificial sweeteners that are poisons for our bodies. Look for natural sweeteners like coconut sugar, maple syrup, stevia, cane sugar, agave, and others.

All in all, incorporating plant-based eating and minimizing packaged food will help you avoid tricky nutrition labels and hidden food additives.

—LOW-GLYCEMIC INDEX—

A way of measuring how fast we digest food and the effect on our blood sugar level. Choosing low glycemic food helps you maintain stable blood sugar levels and prevents diabetes and manages weight.

—GMO—

GMO stands for genetically modified organism. Genetically engineered foods have been altered and include genes that don't naturally occur in foods. I like the joke that GMO means "God Move Over." Sadly, the FDA doesn't require more safety studies unveiling the lies of genetically engineered foods. The movie "Seeds of Death" reveals the dangers of manipulating our foods. Neil Young has even become so angry at the practice that he's released an album called "The Monsanto Years" in his attempt to raise awareness about companies such as Monsanto and Starbucks, which are known to use GMO foods.

Avoid hidden GMO ingredients; there is no national requirement to label GMO foods, only 3 of 50 states in the US require labeling of their packaged foods. Studies revealed that GMO leaves behind harmful material in our bodies linked to cancer, organ damage, infertility, allergies, accelerated aging, and immune disorders. The use of GMOs is a downhill movement. A non-GMO guide and company list is the best way to live GMO-free. The following five foods are known to have the worst affiliation, and you should be aware of them:

- Corn: avoiding corn is a no brainer; many food documentaries have exposed the truth behind GMO corn.
- Soy: Could be in the form of oil, tofu, flour, milk – the majority of these products are genetically modified. So be sure to look for the non-GMO label (see below).
- Sugar: A lot of sugar comes from genetically modified sugar cane or sugar beets. This effects not just pure sugar but any foods with sugar added as an ingredient.
- Cereals: The rice, wheat, and corn that comprise many cereals are often genetically modified, classifying the cereal itself as GMO.
- Cooking oils: corn, canola, soy, and sunflower oil can all be the result of GMO plants and seeds and should be avoided.

—KEEPING AN ALKALIZE BODY—

The human body maintains a delicate pH balance. Too much alcohol, caffeine, meat, dairy, medications and environmental toxins can all mess with your body and its delicate pH balance. If you have too much of this in your diet or life it can create excess acidity in the body. Over time, an overly acidic diet eventually makes our bodies more susceptible to all kind of diseases. Thus, it's imperative that we offset these stressors with superfoods that help us balance our pH levels and alkalize the body.

My favorite way to attack it is with *The Ultimate Elixir*, and the *Ultimate Shrooms*.

The Ultimate Elixir is a green superfood powder. It's made with an alkalizing blend of two dozen nutrient-rich superfoods including barley grass, spirulina, goji, wheatgrass, moringo leaf, reishi mushrooms, kelp, alfalfa, chlorella and chia seeds. The all-organic formula contains zero added sugar or fillers of any kind and it tastes a lot like a beautiful green tea. I start my day with this regimen, taking it in the morning with a glass of water and in less than 30 seconds, I get everything I need to balance my pH and dramatically improve my wellbeing for the day.

Same goes for my coffee ritual alternative or afternoon retreat, I find the Ultimate Shroom powder blend to be the royalty of Chinese medicine with these eight superfood divas; cordyceps, lions maine, chaga, reishi, oyster, turkey tail, maitake, and shitake all condensed into powder, it's considered the caviar of nature and is better than any coffee blend out there.

So you see it's that easy, incorporating good stuff to your diet with benefits like boosting the immune system, lowering cholesterol & blood sugar while sustaining energy & hormonal balance. I don't know of a better choice out there.

Check out the QR code if you'd like to give it a try.

—MY DAIRY DIARY—

For the longest time, I suffered through bloating and discomfort issues. It took me years and many doctors' visits to discover that my problem was due to the consumption of dairy products. Of course, not all dairy products are created equal, but, for years, I've thought that milk was good, it's ingrained in most of us from childhood that we'll have strong bones and get our daily dose of vitamins A, D, and B12.

The truth is that recent studies have shown that milk is only good for babies under three, and, when you think about it, there are no other mammals that consume milk past their youngest years. In truth, the number one protein in milk is casein, the same as glue. Milk is also high in saturated fat and LDL cholesterol. The myth that high milk consumption prevents osteoporosis has largely been dispelled, and, in addition, milk consumption increases the risk of several types of cancer. There are significantly reduced incidences of breast and colon cancer in countries where milk is not a staple in the diet. Asian's don't suffer from western diseases, and I believe it's according to the consumption of milk. 65% of the world population is lactose intolerant, which means they can't even digest the product without getting sick. Since switching from cow milk to almond, and coconut milk, I have no more discomfort– and these milks are just as good in coffee! For some, it's an acquired taste, but once you switch from dairy, you won't want to go back.

—ANOREXIA AND BULIMIA—

Did you know that, according to The National Institute of Mental Health, 1 in 5 women suffer from eating disorders? From childhood, we are conditioned to believe there is an ideal body image. Whether it's *Barbie and Ken*, *The Little Mermaid's* perfect swimsuit figure, or one of the infinite other representations we're exposed to during youth, these influences have a profound effect on our subconscious. The pursuit of a modeling career can exacerbate these already deeply-ingrained body image ideals and cause great insecurity—after all, you're physical appearance is being judged daily. Anorexia and bulimia are two manifestations of these body-image issues that can sneak up on a model, or any entertainer, very quickly.

Anorexia is a lack or loss of appetite for food. It's a serious medical condition brought on by an obsessive desire to lose weight. According to the Department of Health and Human Services, 90% of sufferers are women between the ages of 12-25. Though most anorexic people have no history of being overweight, patients have a distorted mental image of themselves and never feel thin enough. They may exercise excessively and use diuretic pills to lose weight. This disease, if gone unchecked, can result in infinite medical issues ranging from liver disease to heart failure, menstrual irregularities, and nerve damage, among others. Though an anorexic person may lose weight, they also can lose hair, their nails will become brittle, and they'll have an overall unhealthy appearance. This will make it impossible to have a successful modeling career.

Bulimia is a commonly hidden disease. It's harder to identify a bulimic person than a severely anorexic one. Signs of Bulimia include excessive over-eating (3-5 thousand calories within an hour), eating secretly, going to the bathroom immediately after eating (they may run water to cover the sound of vomiting), regular use of laxatives, enemas, and other diuretics, and exercising excessively after a meal. Physical signs of bulimia are knuckle calluses caused by inducing vomiting, chipmunk cheeks, sores in the mouth, dental problems, weight fluctuations, and bloating. Most bulimics have a normal weight but fluctuate depending on the frequency with which they are binging and purging. Bulimia needs to be treated quickly as it is a sometimes fatal condition.

I find it important to include the issue of eating disorders in this book because while the road to a successful modeling career might look glamorous and exciting, you will feel insecure at times when you're rejected for a job or an agency. But there are ways to achieve your goals without falling down the rabbit hole of a disease. I experienced these eating disorders up close and personally as a dancer in Israel. Like modeling, dancing is a very competitive business, and looks do matter. The pressure to remain thin pushed a lot of these teenaged girls into unhealthy eating behaviors.

It was in the early to mid-1990s when there was a sharp increase in cases reported; maybe it has to do with the revelation that some stars and celebrities were willing to take extreme measures, like Princess Diana sharing her courage to combat her eating disorder. This triggered many others to confront their problems and treatment-seeking. It became known as the Diana Effect. In her books, she talks about following a strict diet after the media made comments on her appearance being too "Pudgy. "Once she got in the cycle, she couldn't stop dieting. Of course, the media kept blaming bulimia to be the problem, but Diana insisted that bulimia is only a symptom, and the real problem is the emptiness and void some of us experience at times. In this case, food can become an artificial filler.

Jane Fonda has also publicly discussed her battle with bulimia, which she suffered for 25 years and was initially triggered by the stress of her mother's death. Lady Gaga, Lindsay Lohan, Britney Spears, and many others have spoken out about their struggles, leading to public awareness that has created a decrease in this phenomenon.

Thankfully there has been a light shone on this issue leading many celebrities to discuss their battles with weight and body image distortion. Tyra Banks led the way on her show, America's Next Top Model, mentoring girls to embrace their physique and not be pressured into unnatural methods to achieve an unattainable image.

With the rise of the Kardashian phenomenon, a whole different body parameter was made popular. So much so that Vogue International and other health magazines have agreed not to feature underweight models to encourage the steps to a better self-image and wellness mindset.

—THE ICING ON TOP—

In addition to the essentials for healthy living listed at the beginning of this chapter, I have a few little penchants that keep me feeling and performing at my peak.

—MASSAGE—

My forever "go-to fix." A two hours deep tissue massage. If I happen to go for two weeks without it, it sure takes a toll on my physical and mental well-being. Being a former dancer, I was always very in tune with my body and understood the importance of releasing tension, getting rid of toxins, rejuvenating the chakras, and realigning the body's imbalances. My favorites are deep tissue sports massages, but I've tried them all. Ayurvedic, Thai, Swedish, deep tissue, aromatherapy, shiatsu, and reflexology, are all great options. After traveling extensively through Asia, I became a big believer in their custom of reflexology and massage. Reflexology is not commonly practiced in America, but that's beginning to change as people start to realize the importance of rebalancing the pressure points in your palms, feet, and ears—these areas are maps of your life, and by triggering the right points you can solve a lot of common issues, just like in acupuncture.

—COLONICS—

I'm a big believer in colon hydrotherapy, and I'm not the only one. Kim Kardashian, Opera Winfrey, Paris Hilton, and so many more talk freely about being an advocate for such a regimen. This may not be for everybody, and it's important to know the pros and cons before colonic therapy.

Colonics were originally an Egyptian practice, the purpose being to eliminate waste and disease-causing bacteria from the colon by flushing it with ten liters of water. It can deplete your nutrients, so it's essential to take supplements, enzymes, and probiotics whenever you do the therapy. Dehydration is also an issue, so hydrate, hydrate, hydrate.

After traveling extensively from Indonesia to Thailand, my normal eating habits were off-kilter—air travel and ethnic cuisine had wreaked havoc with my digestive system, so I tried my first colonic. Wow, did I feel amazing! Bloating and constipation were things of the past, and my stomach never looked flatter. I now go every three to six months – always after traveling or when the seasons change. The first time could be intimidating, but it's well worth it. Once you're used to the procedure, it's like getting your teeth cleaned. Since I don't fast, I do colonics; that's my cleanse.

Don't be surprised to find mixed opinions about colonics; many physicians warn against them; however, they are very popular among naturopathic doctors and alternative health practitioners. The benefits were further confirmed to me when I got my certification as a natural health practitioner.

As we all know, achieving a balanced lifestyle takes time, knowledge, and practice. Juggling the emotional, spiritual, mental, physical, and intellectual capacities are art forms on their own. But allowing yourself to live a clean, toxic-free lifestyle should be first and foremost a priority.

There is so much we can do from the inside as well as the outside. Some changes will take time, but once you are aware of them, it will be easier to track them down to cause an action. From quitting smoking, avoiding refined sugars, or heavy alcohol to being overly stressed and neglecting exercise— any change is always a challenge. But I promise that by actively changing bad habits, over time, they'll be replaced by healthier choices. At times, you might feel that you're sacrificing your social life by going to bed early and avoiding the last cocktails or the late-night parties, but, nothing ventured, nothing gained, and your life and career will thrive if you consistently stay focus on your target!

As Muhammad Ali said, "Don't quit, suffer now and live the rest of your life like a champion."

CHAPTER SIX

—EXERCISE—

Since the 1950s, when televisions became a living room staple, we've become a nation of couch potatoes and electronic magnets. Kids used to play outside, riding bikes, hiking, and chasing after balls. These days, it seems that instead of playing the games, we're mostly watching them—becoming increasingly sedentary. This results in ballooning weight, lethargic lifestyles, and the development of disease. Obesity is becoming the norm, according to recent statistics. In American alone, 35.7% of adults and 16.9% of children are considered obese. It is officially defined by having body fat percentage of over 25% for men and boys and 32% for women and girls.

—BMI VS. WEIGHT—

The scale can tell how heavy you are, but how much fat you have. Your indication calculator is the BMI: Body Mass Index. It's very simple to find your BMI:

BMI = Weight in Pounds / Heights in inches x Height in inches x 703

To calculate your BMI, use the chart below and see where you fall.

—BODY FAT PERCENTAGE—

Description	Women	Men
Essential Fat	12-15%	2-5%
Athletes	16-20%	6-13%
Fitness	21-24%	14-17%
Acceptable	25-31%	18-25%
Obese	32%+	25%+

—THE RIGHT EXERCISE FOR YOU—

As a former certified fitness and Pilates instructor, I've seen people go from a mediocre workout on an elliptical to a vigorous fitness routine once they're motivated to try something new or create a noticeable change. Transformation happens when you're fully inspired and dedicated to take the challenge, so finding a workout that gets you motivated is a key element.

Whether it's biking, swimming, dancing, weight training, running, boxing, or other form of exercise, make sure to keep alternating your routine. For me, 3 to 5 workouts a week is sufficient unless I have a lot of fitness work on the horizon, then I push it to 6. As a general rule, I do a minimum of 45 minutes of cardio, followed by 30-45 minutes of weight training. For the first 20 minutes of cardio, I try to raise my heart rate to the maximum, this part of the workout burns sugar, and the remaining cardio starts burning fat. I don't bother with less than 40 to 45 minutes of cardio. If you're one of those who are already in shape and just wish to maintain, an hour workout is usually sufficient, but if you're looking to shed a few pounds, you'll have to sweat it out a bit longer.

Keeping in shape is more than essential in this business, whether you're a fitness model, spokesperson, part, fit or mature model. When competing with your peer group, your peak physical condition can be a major asset.

Thankfully there is a wide variety of exercises to keep your mind and body guessing. Unless you are doing your sport or activity on a professional level, always change it up, or you'll develop the body type of that sport – the broad shoulders of a swimmer or the muscular thighs of a football player. Also keep in mind that the more you can do, the more special skills you'll have to book that job. Throughout my life, I've enjoyed more workouts than I can count – boxing, capoeira, Soul Cycling, ballroom, and belly dancing – you name it I've tried it. My latest favorite workout is aerial acrobatics that combines yoga, dance, and gymnastics all while suspended in the air, working one's body weight against gravity. The following are few, great, fun, and versatile workout options I enjoy:
Aerobics, bicycling, cycling, skiing, zumba, body-sculpting, horseback riding, rock climbing, pilates.

Though I've tried a lot of great workouts through the years, for me, nothing compares to the power of yoga. Perhaps because I'm able to control the intensity and my body conditioning as it changes with time, especially after the few injuries I had in my early dancing years. A good yoga routine can simply follow you through life's stages and strengthen you both physically and mentally. If there is one workout in the world, I won't give up it would be power yoga

—YOGA—

A Handful of Yogalicious Choices

Yoga, for me, is a "hole-in-one" way to stay aligned with my body and mind connection while providing countless health benefits. Decreasing chronic pain, improving sleep patterns, regulating metabolism, and strengthening your core. It's not surprising that it has been around for more than 5,000 years, and its practice gets constant fine-tuning everywhere.

Nowadays, like anything that works well and is loved, there are many types of Yoga classes and new variations popping up in the market every year. Here's a list of the most common and traditional practices:

—HATHA YOGA—

Originated in India in the 15th century. Hatha serves as a base for other types of yoga. Since it's slow-paced, it's a great option for beginners. Hatha includes both breathing and meditation in its practice.

—VINYASA—

A step up from Hatha, Vinyasa uses a series of 12 poses where movement is matched with breathing. This is a more athletic style yoga that began in the 1980s by Westerners. It's known as "flow" yoga because of the constant movement.

—ASHTANGA—

Ashtanga, also known as "power yoga," with fast-paced and vigorous movement. Lunges, push-ups, and strength training are incorporated into the Ashtanga practice.

—IYENGAR—

Founded by B.K.S Iyengar, this practice is nicknamed "furniture" yoga due to the fact that it incorporates props such as straps, blankets, and blocks, to assist body strengthening and precise alignment. Poses are held for more extended periods than most other forms of yoga.

—BIKRAM—

Known as hot yoga, founded by Bikram Choudhury, is traditionally done in a 100-105 degrees Fahrenheit room at 40% humidity. It's a 90-minute practice with 26 basic poses, which are performed twice. The heat loosens the muscles allowing for greater stretch, and the concentration involved in holding poses for an extended time helps you to tighten the muscles.

—JIVAMUKTI—

Jivamukti translates to "liberation while living." This is a physical practice that incorporates spiritual elements and Sanskrit chanting, with ancient scripture references.

—KRIPALU—

This is a three-part practice that seeks to know, accept, and learn your body. Different poses and postures with extensive hold times are incorporated with meditation; the motto is "your body is your leader."

—KUNDALINI—

Founded by Yogi Bhajan, Kundalini is called "the yoga of awareness" and constantly focuses on moving through invigorating poses. This awakens the body and cultivates spiritual consciousness to practice serving others. Sting and Jennifer Aniston are both practitioners of Kundalini Yoga.

My favorite type of yoga is power yoga combination done in a hot room. I enjoy the fact that in 90 minutes, I get to sweat from the cardio impact, gain flexibility and strengthen my core all at the same time – this is an all-in-one workout that covers my cardio and strength training dosage for the day.

—FOAM ADDICT—SORE NO MORE—

Like many dancers, I've always had flare-ups with my lower back. Ever since I discovered the foam roller, it's become my best friend. It offers similar benefits as a deep-tissue or sports massage, but you can do it in the convenience of your own home. It helps in stretching your muscles and tendons and can reach into hidden areas of tightness and scar tissue. For me, it also releases mental tension, making me feel more centered and balanced throughout the day, which has made foam rolling an essential part of my daily routine. Just 10-15 minutes loosens me up and gives me the energy I need for the day. According to a research study published in the Journal of Strength and Conditioning, rolling before and after a workout leads to less post-workout fatigue.

—CHOOSING A ROLLER—

There are different levels of foam rollers, varying in intensity. If you're new to foam rolling start with a softer, less dense roller to ease into the practice. As you grow accustomed to rolling, increase the density to maximize the benefits of deep-tissue foam rolling.

The following are some basic exercises that will lay the groundwork for rejuvenating your body and releasing tension. I recommend using your foam roller first thing in the morning as it invigorates for the day but anytime is fine.

CHAPTER SEVEN

—MIRA'S MOVEMENT ROUTINE —

If you prefer, you can follow this exercise sequence on your device by scanning the code.

EXERCISE 1

A) Begin lying on your yoga mat with the foam roller placed beneath your shoulder blades. Your knees should be parallel, and buttocks raised in the air with glutes tightened.

B) With your hands under your head slide back so the foam massages your lats. Begin lifting your head to create more pressure on the roller.

C) Keep sliding until your glutes touch the floor. Your upper body should contract into a crunch, your feet flexed.

EXERCISE 2

A) Begin in a plank position with the roller under your thighs, just above your knee, with feet suspended in the air. The neck should be in line with your back.

B) Roll backward, extending your arms, allowing the foam to massage your quadriceps.

EXERCISE 3

A) Lay down flat with knees bent and together feet a few inches apart. Insert the foam vertically between your knees and squeeze.

B) Lift your glutes while squeezing your knees, this will work your glutes and hamstrings. Repeat this 10 times.

EXERCISE 4

A) Place your hands on the floor and raise your legs up over your head.

B) Roll back, allowing your knees to come next to your ears, aiming for a 90-degree pretzel angle. Use your hands to push on your back. You may have to turn your head to one side, allowing more space for your body to contort.

C) Roll back into the original position, trying to keep knees close to your face, gradually rolling your vertebrae back to the mat.

EXERCISE 5

A)   Begin in a Downward Dog position. To do this, kneel on all fours with your toes tucked. Contract your core and straighten your legs, lifting your body into an upside-down V.

B)   Pull your body forward into a plank position, and then bring your right foot in between your hands.

C)   Maintaining your leg position, extend your arms overhead into the Warrior 1 position. Repeat with left leg.

EXERCISE 6

A) Lay on your stomach with your hands under your shoulders, forehead on the mat.

B) Push against the mat to fully extend arms, opening your chest into a full Cobra position.

C) Push your buttocks back toward your feet and open your knees, keep arms extended and relax into a child's pose.

EXERCISE 7

A) Begin in plank position with your toes tucked.

B) Use your core to pull forward on your toes. Then return to the original position by pushing heels back. This back and forth motion is great for your abdominal muscles. Aim for 20 repetitions.

EXERCISE 8

A)   Begin in Warrior 1 position with palms together in prayer position.

B)   Twist left and put your right elbow inside the right knee.

C)   Bring your palms together and place the left elbow on the outside of your right knee. These are great stretches for shoulders and obliques.

EXERCISE 9

A) Place your right foot on the floor and extend the left leg behind you with the knee on the mat.

B) Lower hands onto the mat with right leg on outside of the right arm. Lower onto your forearms. This creates a deep stretch in the hip.

C) Dragon Pose. Rest right knee on the floor, stretching your hamstring. Allow left leg to turn in and rest. Bring the weight to the top of your thigh and rest your arms to support the stretch.

EXERCISE 10

A) Start on your knees, creating a triangle between your head and your arms. Tuck toes and raise buttocks, place the right knee on the right elbow and left knee on the left elbow.

B) Slowly raise legs off of elbows, creating a 90-degree angle with knees and elbows.

C) Continue to raise your legs until knees are in line with hips above shoulders to create a perfect line.

—INVERSION THERAPY—

Several years ago, I discovered inversion therapy and am now an enthusiastic devotee. By hanging upside down on the inversion table, the pressure is removed from the space between my spinal discs. Activities like bending, sitting, running, driving, dancing—especially on the heels I'm wearing—can contribute to constant back pain, so by practicing inversions, I feel a dramatic improvement in my back and neck pain. By now, studies have shown that it is not only promoting healthy blood flow, but also improving brain function and the release of neurotransmitters, endorphins, and balance hormones. Not too bad for just going upside-down.

I try to increase my hanging time by a few minutes every session. Usually using a great song, two or three max for my timekeeper.

It has also helped decrease the frequency of my migraines and the overall pressure relief throughout my body. I use *Teeter Hang-Ups,* but there are many different kinds of inversion devices on the market.

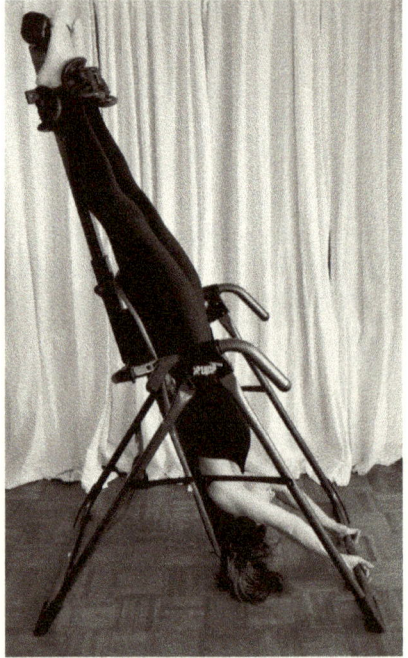

Mira Tzur

CHAPTER EIGHT

—BEAUTY AND MAKEUP—

What is beauty?

By definition, beauty is "a combination of qualities, such as shape, color, or form, that pleases the aesthetic senses, especially the sight." But what is beauty? It's often indescribable, an "it" factor. Other times, it's obvious: a perfectly symmetrical face that turns heads.

The fact is, like love, beauty cannot be defined. There's the external aspect of beauty, but also internal. It's the inner soul, the kindness, passion, fire, or goodness that amplifies an already beautiful face or turns an average one into something amazing. Likewise, dark auras can take an objectively flawless person and reduce them to mediocrity.

In the commercial world, physical perfection is not always required, but positive, vibrant energy is an absolute must—personality is so vital to this spectrum of modeling. On the other hand, fashion modeling focuses solely on the physical, removing the model's individuality from the shoot. Because of the fantasy-like nature of high-fashion photoshoots, there's often a sense of vacancy to the model, a detached other-worldliness.

—MAINTAINING AGELESS BEAUTY—

No one can avoid aging, but aging gracefully is a full-time choice. "Aging is not lost youth but a new stage of opportunity and strength," said writer and activist, Betty Friedan. Getting older is something we all have to face at one point or another. It can be hard to adjust with a mind to the visual reflection pointing to the mirror, and though it can hurt to feel like your time to shine is behind you, that's not necessarily true. Age is just the number of years you've been alive; your quality of life will determine the way age will dress you up. Your potential to stay youthful and radiant is a choice and a constant work in progress. There is no amount of cream or surgery that will fix or cover up the outer layer of someone who isn't beautiful on the inside. We all know there are several known factors that make our skin look older, tired, and lifeless. Age is one of them, but gravity and poor nutrition are also important factors. As we get older, we slowly lose collagen and elastin. After 18, collagen production drops 1% per year and wrinkles, pigmentation, and saggy skin become more present leading us to look tired, older, and even unhappy. Thankfully, there are many ways to bring radiance back.

As a starter, it's good to define your skin type, whether it's dry, oily, or a combination. I love alternating between different kinds of creams as I do with my food intake, versatility is beneficial as long as you're not allergic.

—AGING IS OPTIONAL—

When does one need to go under the knife? This is a topic of constant debate, but I strongly believe that we project what we feel, and if one is not happy about certain physical attributes, it's important to fix them sooner rather than later. When people have characteristics that they find unattractive or are embarrassed by, they can develop lifelong scars that inhibit their day-to-day lives. Why suffer from anxiety and insecurity when in the modern age, a fix is so readily available? How many times have you seen someone instinctively cover their mouth when they laugh because of crooked teeth or turn their head at a certain angle because their wide nose embarrasses them? These are fixable characteristics that cause unnecessarily low self-esteem that can remain over a lifetime, especially during adolescence, when our individuality begins to take shape. My personal opinion is, once someone is fully developed physically, if they are still ashamed of a feature, it's ok to consider changing it. However, if there is any hesitation, hold off on the surgery to get a few opinions because in many cases procedures can now be done without going under the knife. If you know, 100%, that this is a feature you want to change, then there's no point in waiting. However, when considering surgery, it is imperative to fully understand the motivations behind that decision. Is there a societal fad that you want to follow; Kim Kardashian's booty? Or an objectively unattractive feature that is causing emotional discomfort? For adolescents, it's very important that parents help coach them through this decision helping them understand the needs and motives of their children without harboring judgment.

There are also cases where what could be considered a flaw—like Cindy Crawford's mole, Madonna's tooth gap (diastema), or Jennifer Grey's larger nose from her Dirty Dancing days—actually become their moneymakers. A unique feature that sets them apart from the crowd. Grey has repeatedly noted her regret at having a nose job and has claimed it cost her work.

Other, less invasive cosmetic procedures like Botox and fillers are also open for debate. Gravity's effects can start to show on facial skin as early as your '20's and 30's. By using Botox fillers for your face and maintaining youthful skin, you're able to take preventative measures that ensure fewer wrinkles and greater radiance.

Study after study shows that collagen production peaks around 20, and it's a downhill slope from there. Skin plumping creams can only do so much, and many dermatologists recommend beginning injections at the first sign of aging. For some women with good genetics and healthy habits, this may not happen until their 40's. For others, it could be as early as their 20's. By not allowing the skin to sag, you prevent it from happening at all. Once the skin has already begun drooping or the wrinkles have set, the results from injections will be less satisfactory.

Carmen Dell' Orefice, liberatingly admits to enhancing her cheekbones with silicone injections, something she's been doing for decades, as well as using medical dermabrasion therapies. Hence the reason, at 88 years old, she's still landing magazine covers.

Your ethnic origin will dictate the type of skin and reveal the hereditary conditions synonymous within your ethnicity. Ethnic characteristics are just one factor, like diet, menstrual cycle, adequate hydration, and cleansing habits, all affecting your complexion. Since the skin is the largest organ of our body, with its derivatives like hair, nails, glands, and nerve endings, It is imperative to nourish such and make it a prioritized investment.

Fair skin is light and sun-sensitive, often characteristic of Caucasians and some light-skinned Asians and Latinas. Fair skin tends to be drier and is at high risk for sun damage. Be sure to use SPF and, if you do get sun spots, use microdermabrasion to help speed up cell turnover and clear your complexion. Often, fair skin means sensitive skin. If this is the case for you, try calming products like chamomile lotions that soothe the skin and prevent redness and irritation.

Medium skin generally is found on people in the Middle East, East Asia, the Mediterranean, and Latin countries. Individuals with "olive" complexions fall under this category. Medium skin is less sun-sensitive than fair skin but tends to be oilier, which can result in breakouts. If you're medium skinned, be gentle when dealing with breakouts and use a wash that contains salicylic acid. Often, olive complexions are at a higher risk of developing dark spots from pimple pinching, so it may be necessary to use a skin lightening cream or concealer to cover these areas.

Dark-skinned people generally come from Africa, the Caribbean, and Southern Asia. The least sun-sensitive of the skin types, dark skin is less prone to show early signs of aging, that's the good news. The bad news is this skin type can be prone to breakouts and leave behind acne scars. Again, if you suffer from this, wash diligently with salicylic acid cleanser and spot treat break out areas, making sure to moisturize afterward.

—THE UGLY SIDE OF BEAUTY—

Once you determine your skin type you can use products to help you battle father-time. But be careful, not all beauty products are created equal. In fact, the FDA has found mercury, lead, formaldehyde, and carbamide— which is a delicate way of saying animal urine—in lipsticks, anti-aging creams, lotions, and other beauty products.

The truth is, it has been 80 years since congress last voted to regulate cosmetics. So, even well-known companies are getting away with putting harmful chemicals and ingredients in products we use every single day. Of course, this is a huge problem because our skin is our largest organ. It only takes 26 seconds for these toxins to sink into our skin and absorb into our bodies.

There is, however, good news. There are companies standing up and creating products that make our skin feel and look younger without putting our health at risk. I personally use the Live Ultimate Skincare line. It's one of the safest skincare lines on the market and it's EWG Verified.

In case you didn't know, the Environmental Working Group is the leading advocate in skin safety and education. In the US, they have only approved about 100 companies and Live Ultimate Skincare collection is one of those companies. Beyond being EWG verified, it contains ingredients that have been clinically tested and proven. They were designed for all skin types and humans including both men and women. This skincare line is certified organic, cruelty free, GMO free, certified vegan—no crushed up beetles or whale vomit here—and most important; made in the USA in a CGMP certified facility. But here's the thing; these products aren't just safe, they actually work!

To learn more about the Live Ultimate Skincare Collection Scan This Code Here.

If the universal law of polarity is true, then all things beautiful have a diametrically opposite side of them. In hopes to satisfy the insatiable desire to look beautiful, we assume that the only price we are paying for a product or procedure is money. If you look closer, the entire industry has been an offender against mother nature and beauty itself. Most products on the market contain toxic, cancer causing, hormone disrupting ingredients that get absorbed into our bloodstream and cause serious health problems. We tend to put blind trust in brands that, in fact, care about their bottom lines and their expenses go into marketing and package design rather than sourcing the purest and cleanest ingredients possible. It is our duty to take responsibility for investigating and protecting our health by knowing for sure what it is that we are putting in and on our bodies. Dare to ask bigger questions of product makers, demand transparency, and vote with your dollars.

—LENA KAPTEIN—

Hair & Makeup Interview

Q: How long have you been doing Hair and Makeup to accompany your modeling and family photography business?

A: I started doing makeup 20 years ago, transitioning into being a makeup artist after years of modeling.

Q: What are the main differences when applying makeup?

A: The main difference when applying makeup is to first look at the person's skin texture and color, and then face shape. That will determine what type of makeup and how to apply the makeup.

Q: What are some of your favorite companies and products you use and swear by; your secret regimen?

A: These are just a few of my favorite brands in my kit; *Armani, Bravon Beauty, Charlotte Tilbury, Hourglass, Laura Mercier, MAC, Makeup Forever*. There are a lot of great brands out there, and I find great things in each one.

These are products that I regularly use on clients; *Makeup Forever HD foundation, MAC* face and body foundation & blot powder, *Nars* concealer, and their bronzing powder in Laguna, Laura Mercier's *Secret Camouflage* and loose setting powder. *Bravon Beauty* blushes and lip glosses, *Charlotte Tilbury Bronze and Glow* and lip liner in pillow talk, *Armani* silk foundation, *Hourglass* powders.

Q: How should a model arrive at a casting and her actual shoot day—anything to prepare the evening before or the morning of?

A: Models should arrive at a casting with natural/ minimal makeup. If needed, light cover-up under eyes and on the skin if blotchy or any breakouts. Curled lashes with a little bit of mascara. If pale, just a bit of bronzing powder and blush. Lip balm as needed. Clients don't want to see makeup, so make sure all is blended well.

The day of the booking, arrive with 8 hours of sleep and clean face no makeup on, only moisturizer. Make sure your lashes are without yesterday's mascara and eyeliner. Always manicured hands and feet and no tan lines on your body. Well-groomed too, of course.

Q: What are current makeup trends or some of your must-haves?

A: Current makeup trends are still contouring and using highlighters to minimize and enlarge specific areas of the face. Eyebrows are sculpted yet more natural, fuller shapes. Everyone wants to have bigger pouty lips. Winged eyeliners with individual lashes to make eyes appear bigger and lifted.

Must-haves are concealer, mascara, a lash curler, a translucent setting powder, a taupe eyeshadow, cream blush, and a bronzer.

Q; What are your top tips for healthy skin—do's and don'ts

A: Your skin is a reflection of your lifestyle, so make sure you follow these tips:

Get a good night's sleep, exercise every day, drink a lot of water, and eat live foods. Wear a sunscreen every day and make sure you use a good moisturizer. Clean your face every night using gentle products. Exfoliate dry skin and use masks to keep your skin healthy and smooth. Your skin is your work, so treat it well and protect it. Never get a facial treatment the day before a booking, unless it's a mask you have used before. You may get a reaction, or your skin may be sensitive to wearing makeup the next day. No waxing on face day before a shoot. Never tan your face or use self-tanning products.

Q; Do you have pet peeves when models are sitting in the chair?

A: Texting and being on your phone looking down unless necessary and business-related. Being sick, coughing, or constantly wiping your nose. Eating or chewing gum. Talking and laughing with another model while getting their lips or eye makeup done.

Q: Name a few of your favorite jobs, models, and fun or embarrassing situations.

A: Favorite jobs are beauty campaigns and shoots where I get to create looks that the average person won't wear. I love the shoots we do in our studio where we can customize each model's portfolio shoot, and I get to create all different looks on each model from very organic to high fashion looks.

CHAPTER NINE

—MOTIVATION & INSPIRATION—
COPING WITH REJECTION

As attractive as this business looks from the outside looking in, becoming a model won't happen overnight. Creating a professional and presentable portfolio with versatile images is the foundation to get you out, like a resume or CV in other professions. You must be prepared for some rejection as you will not be able to book every job, get every callback, or may not even get the initial phone call for the castings out there. It is essential that you understand your core strengths and unique attributes. Your self-esteem and self-confidence must be a higher priority than booking the job.

Think of it this way. To my son, I'm a mom; to some, I'm a friend, for others, a co-worker. In a casting, they are looking for you to be a particular person, maybe on that day, they don't see you as that person—don't take offense at this, it's just the way someone perceives you at that given moment or an indescribable chemistry that determines whether you're a fit for the project or not.

Our perceptions of ourselves might be the complete opposite of how others see us. Thus, it's essential to do your homework in knowing yourself to create a complete, well-rounded package for your agent to market you. When I counsel newcomers to the industry, I recommend they write their expectations and goals for the next one, two, and five years in this business. It's good to be as specific as possible, so I have them research the types of jobs they'd like to book, the kinds of agents they'd like representing them, the lifestyle they want to create, and the sacrifices they're willing to make. There's nothing you can't achieve; the question is; how much are you willing to give? There is a great saying, "If you want a hard life, do easy things now, if you want an easy life, do hard things now ".

—EMBRACING YOUR TRANSITIONS—

Certain skills that used to come naturally to me no longer do. I realized that, in my 40's, some physical abilities that were once assets, such as my contortion skills, were no longer possible. It was a tough thing to accept. That asset, my ace in the hole, was no longer my first card to flaunt.

When I studied Kabbalah, one of the first things they taught was don't open the Zohar (the book on which Kabbalah is based) until you're 40 because you have no tools to "get it". The 20 or 30 something mind doesn't have the experience to understand these teachings. Well, after 40, I've learned that while my body may not contort quite the way it did, it can still do more yoga and fitness than many of my 30-something peers. By accepting this fact I've remained ahead of the curve, rather than trying to fit a square peg in a round hole, I found a round peg. Everybody says 40 is over the hill. What's over the hill? A valley, a trophy, the holy grail, or an aha moment? Whatever it is, think of it as education. You've got your college degree in life; now it's time for your masters.

Age is a funny concept, especially in this business. As a little kid, I remember bragging about the "fraction" ages. Every three months I was that much closer to another birthday. As we get older, we're shy to reveal our real age like it's a price tag or something. Who decides what's a desirable age? I've seen women reach their 80's or 90's and, rightfully, again start bragging about those fraction milestones, wearing them like a badge of honor.

When life expectancy was 60, of course, 40 seemed old. But now I look at hitting 40 or 50 as obtaining a Ph.D. All those years spent learning, create a knowledge base necessary for life—at 40, you're on a new platform, those previous years of education and experience manifesting themselves into your higher purpose, both personally and professionally.

You may be surprised how many household names didn't "make it" until they became quadragenarians. Henry Ford spent his first 40 years studying and practicing engineering but didn't start the *Ford Motor Company* until after his 40th birthday, and he changed the world.

Dame Judy Dench spent years as a theater actress but didn't become a household name until *Golden Eye* was released in 1995. She was 60 years old. Since then, she won an Oscar and has been nominated multiple times. We'd all be missing out had she quit the industry at 40.

Morgan Freeman is known to nearly everyone for his stellar acting skills and deep voice, but it wasn't until Driving Miss Daisy—which was released when Freeman was 52—that the actor became a household name. So now you see, it only gets better after 40.

Look at models; so many women spend years in this business learning how to manage themselves as professionals while maintaining their physical appearance. Why stop at 40 because of industry stereotypes? Make 50, 60, 70, 80, and even 90—ages to aspire to and to be a physical manifestation of inner and outer beauty. For many women, the best is yet to come.

These days, with life expectancy reaching all-time highs—according to the CDC, it's currently 78.8 years in the US—and that's just an average, so imagine the number of people reaching 100. Soon, centenarians will be the norm.

It perplexes me that, in this business, people are often considered examples when they're young but not when they're older. If example equals model in a dictionary, shouldn't you be an example when you're older? Where does it say you have to stop? A beautiful, well-preserved older woman is a work of art, while a beautiful young woman is a work of nature. One is given, the other is worked for.

I will never forget about this girl I was mentoring who wanted to copy the same shoot I had done. She's beautiful, younger, and very fit. We built the sets to be identical to my photoshoot and used the same photographer. But she had little experience and didn't know how to pose and work her angles, even if I put her in the exact position. It all came down to experience and confidence built with time. In-person she was stunning, but in photos, she didn't have the experience to perfect those shots. Experience and beauty are not equal. Sometimes, oddly enough, experience is more important than beauty. Nowadays, little details like a small frown line or eye color can be retouched in postproduction, but the composition of the shot, the message her body depicts, or nailing the perfect facial expression, cannot be edited.

—MEDITATION & SPIRITUAL PRACTICE—

For some of us, meditation goes hand in hand with spiritual or religious practice. Many religions, from Buddhism to Islam and Christianity to Judaism, use meditation or prayer to reflect upon and deepen the meaning of God's word. However, meditation doesn't have to be attached to religion and is often used for personal self-reflection for those seeking peace of mind and clarity.

There's no "right way" or one universal way to approach meditation; there are many different types and styles, and since, as humans, we aren't created equal, it's a personal journey, and over time, meditative practices are honed to fit your individual needs. That said, if you're just getting started, here are a few common methods of meditation I happened to explore and can make it easier for you to compare:

- **Chanting & mantra-based meditation:**
  Buddhism uses concentration and mantras to focus the mind in a singular place. The intent is to cut out unnecessary noise and fully focus inward. This didn't quite grab me after several attempts since I had a problem repeating a phrase that didn't make sense in translation. The repetition is the essence of the practice.

- **Mindfulness:**
  A 2000 year old meditation tradition created by Buddhists and commonly used worldwide in yoga practices. It has easier access since not one organization is behind it. It also has no set cost or rules to enjoy this practice, although it is recommended you practice for two minutes daily. The premise is to fully take in the space surrounding you, appreciating the environment you're in, as you

become it, finding center and a sense of place, using breath, sensation, awareness, and focus. Encouraging the cultivation of nonjudgment, moment by moment, awareness during practice and in everyday life—My favorite program.

- **Transcendental Meditation:**
  This Hindu practice was created in the fifties. It is A privately held, closed system you can only learn from an authorized TM teacher through the initiation ceremony. You'll be required to practice twice a day for 20 minutes and your mantra must remain secret—digging deep to find a place where the mind is both silent and fully alert. This will allow you to achieve clarity while calming the mind.

My meditative practice goes hand in hand with yoga. I like the feeling of my body and mind intertwining, finding a balance between the two. This is a constant work in progress for me, but I find the process of meditation incredibly enlightening and invigorating. It sets me on a positive path for the remainder of the day by consciously eliminating my negative thoughts and calming my sometimes scattered mind.

Mindfulness is my go-to tool. Ironically, the more hectic my day is, the more I need to stop and take that twenty-minute meditation break. I may not think there's the time, but that one step back sends me two steps forward. By opening my 7 Chakras to a new flow of energy and clarity, I get a system reboot, just like my computer rebooting itself daily.

Many people are skeptical about meditation in general but give it a try anyway and reap the benefits. The only skeptics I've met are those who have never tried it. Thich Nhat Hanh, a Vietnamese Buddhist monk, sums it up well: "Meditation is not to escape from society but rather to come back to ourselves and see what is going on. Once there is 'seeing,' there must be acting".

—Either the end or the beginning. It's up to you—

With love,
Mira

Mira Tzur

THANK YOU

First of all, thank you to my wonderful parents, equally beloved, who have granted me with a wonderful, healthy upbringing, incredible set of values, authentic choices, and the freedom to develop my personality, even with my unique traits and, at times, rebellious character. For always supporting me in my journey, showering me with love and comfort, dedicating their life to the well-being of my sister and for me. For sticking by each other always and showing us your unconditional love, and marriage's core-values, till the end.

My late mother, Yafa Zur, whom I lost two years ago after a long battle with cancer. My love, my gratitude, my appreciation, and the fundamental memories I hold deeply in my heart. I will forever cherish your soul, and you will forever be a significant part of me.

My father, Yehuda Zur, who remains, holding the family together, year after year, having no regard for the obstacles and health hazards, one punch at a time and remaining the bionic man in the family. I'll always cherish your unconditional care for Mom as she started deteriorating, slowly, from the disease, and your precious love for each other till her very last breath. For your continued support for aunt Bruria who contributes to the harmony, and most of all, for being my best friend and my rhyme and reason, teaching me as a young girl the valuable life lessons, such as: Always telling the truth, so you won't need to remember your lies, when upset, count to ten before you reply—ok, maybe eleven, blood isn't water, family is everything, your word is your bond, everything will be ok by tomorrow. Well, he actually said, It'll be ok by the time you get married, but that's for another entire book about my relationships.

My one & only. My beloved Son, Alon (Tzur) Berkowitz—the soul that keeps elevating everything worth doing and everything worth fighting for in my life. For your focus and direction, athletics, wit, and intelligence, for always taking the lead and working hard to achieve your goals and make a difference. I can't wait to do a bedtime story with you all over again.

My sister, Sharon, who has been a true angel in my life. The most protective and supportive sister one could ask for. Always listening and ready to help out. Together with your husband, Avi Zohar, you became observant and Orthodox Jews right after marriage. Although that was in my late twenties, by doing so, and after a long period of resentment, you shared with me the beautiful light and great values that our beautiful religion sets in place, something I'll always enjoy yet keep challenging.

My beautiful nieces, Shira, and Yael Zohar, who are a beacon of light in our family; filed with an abundance of love, wisdom, and purity that is rare to find.

My Extended family, friends, agents, clients, and team who supported me through my personal growth and business endeavors. In good times and in bad, through multiple careers in which I have been happily participating.

And last but not least, For all my husbands, boyfriends, and lovers. Those who came to my life and those who I haven't had the pleasure to know yet; Let the past bring the present of a miraculous magical future.

Together, you've been instrumental in the making of Mira and what she may become tomorrow.

Finally, thank you for all who have contributed to the making of this book. There are so many wonderful individuals I wanted to include, but with time running out and the world changing before our eyes, I'm positive that we will continue the journey on learning this business further via live interviews and panel discussions. Thank you again to everyone who helped make this manual a community guide for an industry that I love, and hope will last forever!

*"You can't go back and change the beginning, but you can
start where you are and change the ending."*
~ C.S. Lewis.

ABOUT THE AUTHOR

Mira Tzur is best known for her multi-faceted talents and familiar presence. She is an Israeli-American actress, theater, and film producer, a French countess from the Theraube lineage, social philanthropist, and selectively serves as the #1 FLOTUS impersonator.

But this is only a small segment of her rich and diversified life. Born and raised in Herzliya, Israel, Ms. Tzur began her first career as a prodigy ballet and musical theatre performer, graduating Thelma Yellin School of the Arts with a full scholarship from the America-Israel Cultural Foundation (AICF) she joined the world-renowned Batsheva Dance Ensemble and shortly after was drafted to the Israeli Defense Force to serve her country, as a counterintelligence officer.

Relocating to New York City, Ms. Tzur continued her studies at the Lee Strasberg Institute, NYU Film, and Atlantic Theater school. She appeared in the national Broadway touring company of Cabaret and Cleopatra.

Following her move to Monte Carlo as a resident artist, she performed at the royalty Sporting Theatre, for series of concerts with Elton John, Liza Minnelli, Harry Connick Jr, Julio Iglesias, Paul Anka, and many others throughout Europe & the US Her original choreography of the famous Gypsy Jezebel led to her next royalty performance invite for King Hassan II palace theater in Marrakech Morocco.

Ms. Tzur speaks four languages: English, Hebrew, Arabic, and Yiddish.

Her first segue from the theatre was the television series on Comedy Central Viva Variety directed by Mark Gentile, followed by recurring roles on *FX's Rescue Me* with Denis Leary, *NBC's 30 Rock* with Alec Baldwin, *Fox's Fringe* by J.J. Abrams, *HBO's How to Make it in America* by Mark Wahlberg, *Oxygen's* Body of Work, *Bravo's Untying the Knot*. Her film credits include: *The Stepford Wives, The Devil Wears Prada, Pink Panther, The Last Dance, Junk, My Father My Don*, Slovenian Lady Land Documentary, *Hardly Waiting*.

Throughout her ongoing career, Tzur's face and voice have been associated with countless national Tv commercials and ad campaigns including *Neutrogena, Mary Kay, Ponds, Head and Shoulders, L'Oreal, Hilton, Four Season, Viagra, Advil, Humira, Cool Sculpting, Eskata, Electrolux, Samsung, Sony, Sub Zero, DropBox, Foxwoods, Bank of America, Citibank, US Bank, Macy's, Lazy Boy, Home Depot, Vitamin Shoppe, Campbell's, Ray-Ban, Nike, Reebok, DKNY, Capelli,* and many more.

In 2011 Mira founded *One Circle Productions*. With a keen eye for great stories, talent, and the ability to raise capital, she fosters projects that are thought-provoking, reflective, and socially responsible—promoting diverse voices.

Mira's philanthropy work continues as the Director of I-PEARLS, an aid organization for victimized children with burn injuries. As an advisory committee for America Israel Culture Foundation, and as the Ambassador of the Bali Children Project,

Mira continues to assist in raising awareness and support through her vast network and resources.

www.ingramcontent.com/pod-product-compliance
Lightning Source LLC
Chambersburg PA
CBHW021332090426
42742CB00008B/574